S#125687

C

UCF

D1474283

Early Reform in American Higher Education

Early Reform in American Higher Education

David N. Portman
SYRACUSE UNIVERSITY

Foreword by Alan P. Splete

Professional Technical Series

Nelson-Hall Company Chicago

ISBN: 0-911012-41-9

Library of Congress Catalog Card Number: 72-186982

Nelson-Hall Company, Publishers
325 Jackson Boulevard, Chicago, Illinois 60606

Manufactured in the United States of America

Contents

SECTION II: ADMINISTRATIVE ASPECTS

Acknowledgements

Preparing a page of acknowledgement surely must be one of the more satisfying exercises for a writer. It generally means the main body of research and writing is finished, and for the first time in many months he can relax and reflect upon the effort. It is also, without doubt, the easiest section to write because, at this point, gratitude is pouring out of his pen. It is with pleasure, therefore, that I pay my respects to the following individuals.

Without detailing particular contributions, I owe a great, if somewhat indirect, debt to Maurice Troyer of Syracuse University whose respect for and encouragement of individuality stands high among his virtues. Thanks should also be accorded to Allen Splete, Vice-President of St. Lawrence University, who some years ago kindled my interest in the subject and who was kind enough to contribute a foreword to the book. Additionally, the fruit of my work might not have been achieved without the advice at critical moments of Robert Mickler, also of Syracuse University.

Special thanks go to my wife Lois, for her patience and encouragement and for finding time she did not have to help with the proofs.

I dedicate this book to my sons Douglas and Eric. While they will only read about this first reformation of American higher education they will surely live through the second.

Foreword

Writing this foreword is indeed a pleasure. A teacher is always honored when one of his students becomes stimulated by something he is trying to convey. In this instance it was the importance of studying the history of American higher education in order to gain a perspective through which to study contemporary problems. Mr. Portman's interest in the history of higher education was evident when he was a student. This collection is part of his search to bring up past ideas for fresh review; and, I hope, it represents only the beginning of that quest.

The essays in this collection represent the educational convictions of "early reformers" in the post Civil War period. One need only review the titles included to see how current their focus remains.

Charles W. Eliot in "What Is A Liberal Education?" questions the significance of the bachelor of arts degree in 1884. It is still being questioned today. Eliot advocates a change in the traditional course of study of the day by demonstrating a need to reflect new areas of study.

The mechanism for this change was equal recognition for courses in English, French, German, History, Political Economy and Natural Science. These were to be elevated to same plateau as the revered Greek, Latin and Math courses of the day. In Eliot's view, the entrance of these new, relevant subjects to the magic circle of the liberal arts would permit new and old courses to engage in fair competition.

The problems about academic options and the choice of coordinate studies for students that Eliot discussed are vivid today. Responses to them can be seen in increased student flexibility on all educational levels and in a lessening emphasis on traditional requirements. The modification of the order of studies, which course should come first and why, continues to be of interest in 1972. Eliot's insights relate to the status of the bachelor of arts degree and what it means—the search for this answer appears unchanged in its intensity.

In "Must The Classics Go?" Andrew West reminds us of the importance and value of studying classics. A renewed interest on the part of many contemporary institutions in a classics program means that many will find a source of support in his cogent defense of the classics as the crucial part of a liberal education.

West states that *only* Greek and Latin can provide that mental discipline and the thinking in terms of causal relationships essential to the development of an informed person. In his opinion, the classics accomplish this in a more superior manner than math and science.

A scarcity of "good" classic teachers still exists and, as West notes, speaks to its demise as an important aspect of a liberal arts curriculum.

West points out in his second contribution, "What Is Academic Freedom?" the folly of comparing the American college with the German university. In his view, conditions in the two countries were too dissimilar to permit an imitation—American college students were less mature than their German counterparts, and the preparatory education in America was not equivalent to the gymnasium experience. The elective and free approach of the German university could not be accepted if the discipline of character, a hallmark of American colleges, was to be upheld.

Richard Ely in his article, "American Colleges and German Universities," illustrates the basic differences between the two institutions and questions whether colleges could ever assume a university status. The German university was viewed as a school that prepared students to pass established examinations for entrance into a profession. Studies were elective and optional in that system.

The American college is not a university in Ely's eyes but rather the equivalent of a gymnasia where general intellectual training was to be obtained. It provided a course of study for general culture not professional training. Further, Ely states that the requirements for American teachers were too low, the costs of American education too high and that a great city was the only place for a true university. German universities had high standards for their teachers, provided an education at reasonable costs and situated themselves in urban areas.

This comparison reminds us that labeling classical colleges as universities when it was fashionable and prestigious to do so is very misleading if one accepts the characteristics of the German university defined above.

Gilman in "The Idea of the University" makes us aware of the blurring distinctions between the roles of colleges and universities in America. He envisions them as having different functions, the college as preparation for the university where lessons of discipline are acquired as a springboard to true intellectual freedom.

Be he in a college or university, this great reformer reminds us that the professor represents the heart of any institution of higher learning. Although differentiating between the role a faculty member performs at the two institutions, the essential conditions for developing successful teachers spelled out by Gilman are still applicable: leisure to reflect, service to students, a means of publication, instruments for pursuit of his interest and pay to allow maximum time for work. To Gilman an excellent teacher was one who was always learning and represented a living example of this to students.

David Starr Jordan in "Pettifogging Law-Schools and an Untrained Bar" openly criticizes the post Civil War professional training in law. He indicates that the law faculty must be a part of the university faculty and the law department must have equal status with all other departments, if necessary competence is to be attained. Lawyers needed a general education, Jordan noted, more than any other segment of society, since they represent much of our ruling body. George E. Howard eloquently states the case for state universities in America in 1891. His article, "The State University in America," includes an important historical review of the legislation leading to a wide acceptance of "popular education." Shortening undergraduate courses, as he suggests, "to facilitate earlier entrance into the professions" is once again, in 1972, a subject of considerable interest.

Howard characterizes the state university as a unique "American" institution where ideas such as secularization, coeducation, non-residency, a state educational system and direct service to society are held high. One wonders if these traits are still as visible in contemporary state universities and if they are pursued with the same intensity as in 1891. This is an important question since state universities may have assumed new guidelines to accommodate the large student enrollments of the 1960's.

W. T. Hewett in his article "University Administration" appears to be a forecaster and realist. In the former capacity, he envisioned composition of governing boards and relationship of faculty to general administration to be key questions in resolving the lack of uniformity in administration. These still rate high in governance suggestions and solutions of 1972.

References to alumni mail balloting as a means to secure outside participation, the need for Faculty Senates, the meaning and value of degrees and departmental organization demonstrate that past concerns are still present.

E. R. Sill's "Shall Women Go to College?" is very appropriate in a day of women's liberation. His advocacy of the right of women to a higher education by virtue of equality in the development of intelligent minds dispels the fanciful notions of the period that women should not be allowed to go to college. Courageously, he moves beyond that to state both sexes should receive their college training together breaking down provincialism. The naturalness of a complete college family with daily contact of differing points of view is still a convincing argument for residential, coeducational institutions and sheds some light on why more colleges have been considering or have decided to go coed recently.

Harriet Beecher Stowe's historical summary in "The Education of Freedman" is an outstanding piece of research. The reader is led in vivid detail through a list of religious-educational contributions to the education of the freedman and a brief description of the unique characteristics and contribution of Howard, Berea, Fisk and Hampton Colleges.

Of great significance is Berea's recognition that it was impossible to educate the races separately and still expect blacks to receive first class citizenship and respect. We would all do well to record permanently Stowe's remark "Class prejudices can not be legislated away, but they can be educated away." What an eloquent testimony of fact fit for all ages.

The concluding article in this collection, an anonymous piece entitled "Chautauqua Local Circles and Summer Assemblies," depicts in depth the workings of the Chautauqua Literary ard Scientific circles. These circles portray the extension, adult and continuing education of the period in its finest sense. One is impressed with the organization of summer assemblies, the use of visiting lecturers, and the range and scope of academic and religious areas covered.

It is noted that over 20,000 individuals had graduated from the Chautauqua plan by 1889. This attests to its dynamism and appeal. Current trends in 1972 toward self-learning and external degrees reflect the "raison d' etre" for Chautauqua's extension education plan — allowing individuals to pursue what they wish and to facilitate that pursuit.

A careful reading of these eleven articles reveals that the history of higher education is a valid resource for understanding present problems. There is something for everyone interested in the educational history of the post Civil War period in this collection. Its significance will be determined by the use that concerned students of higher education make of it.

Allen P. Splete
St. Lawrence University
Canton, New York

Early Reform in American Higher Education

Introduction

The several decades after the Civil War witnessed a vital national debate in American higher education. Though the roots of reform have been traced back into earlier periods of American history, it was only after the Civil War that the attention of the public was, in a national sense, directed to the issues. During this era educators were concerned with such issues as the expanding curriculum, electives, professional education, education for those not drawn from the traditionally schooled classes, as well as student activity and behavior.

It has been shown by a variety of researchers that an observer of the American University of 1900 would find virtually unrecognizable, by any standard, the colleges before the war. "The decades after 1865 saw a definite process of metamorphosis, operating on many levels, occur within what was an already venerable corner of American life. Despite significant elements of continuity in that change, the college scene before 1865 seems archaic indeed when set against the new and rapidly working forces of academic reform."*

The rapid proliferation of popular and literary journals of the period provided reformers and traditionalists with a means of carrying the debate to the people. It is not suggested here

---

* Laurence R. Veysey, *The Emergence of the American University* (Chicago: The University of Chicago Press, 1965), p. 2.

that without these journals ideological confrontation and reform would not have taken place. It is proposed, however, that through popular journalism, interest in the issues was stimulated and may well have accelerated the pace of reform in a number of areas including the role of women in higher education as well as university extension. It at least provided college leaders with a popular platform from which to rationalize and sell their views.

This book assumes, or at least hopes, that the reader will be familiar with Rudolph, Brubacher and Rudy, Veysey, or any one of several general period histories of the American college and university. In varying degrees, these histories provide a useful context for this collection of essays.

It should be further pointed out that with one exception (Number 11) every essay contained in this book appears in exactly the form intended by its author. For a number of reasons there have been no other cutting, change of language, or alteration of any kind. First, the reader is provided with the author's view of the issues in their original context. Secondly, the literary style is preserved and provides the reader with a feeling for the "tone" of the period. As a result, the articles vary somewhat in pace, and while for the most part they show internal unity, diversity is their chief characteristic. If, in fact, this is a flaw, the editor hopes it is one with which the reader can live.

The eleven articles selected for this book are somewhat arbitrarily divided into two sections, the first based on curricular matters and the second on administration. The editor acknowledges that for a number of these essays this line of distinction is thin indeed. In these cases, particularly in Section One, placement was assigned on a "building block" manner.

The primary issue of the post-Civil War period was curricular and involved German influence on the American college. Charles William Eliot, one of the truly remarkable men in the history of higher education in America, president of Harvard for forty years, became perhaps the most influential

18

and famous educator of his era. Although he demonstrated concern for a broad range of problems including those of secondary and professional education, Eliot led the fight for undergraduate academic reform. During his reign the elective principle came to dominate Harvard and achieve national visibility. In the article included here, Eliot discusses defects of the traditional curriculum and presents his version of reform.

In defense of the classics, Andrew West, a professor of Latin at Princeton who in later years was appointed dean of that institution's graduate school, waged ideological battle with Eliot in a series of journal articles published during the 1880's. It was West's fear that introduction of an expanded curriculum and freedom of choice at an early age would undermine and eventually force out the classics.

Richard Ely, a political economist trained in Germany who distinguished himself as a scholar and teacher at Johns Hopkins and the University of Wisconsin, clarifies the curricular issue by comparing at length the German University and the American college, emphasizing their points of difference and incompatability. The idea of a university—what it ought to be—is the subject of Daniel Coit Gilman's essay. Five years prior to writing this essay Gilman had been recommended by White of Cornell, Angell of Michigan, and Eliot of Harvard for the leadership of the new Johns Hopkins University. As a distinctly graduate institution Johns Hopkins, under Gilman, was to have a profound effect on American higher education. The first section closes with a commentary by David Starr Jordan on the inadequate preparation for the practice of law, and the sad state of professional education generally. In 1889, after serving several years as president of Indiana University, Jordan began a long and troubled career at Stanford University.

While the prospect of a broadened curriculum and specialized study was the central issue of the period and received the greatest attention, other reforms were being effected. Section Two deals with a number of issues in administrative reform including the growth of the state university and the extension of college level work to accomodate groups which had generally been denied access to higher education in America.

Until the Civil War, Negroes had been prohibited by law in many states from learning to read and write. Through the Freedmen's Bureau an educational system was established in the South and Harriet Beecher Stowe, in a series of articles commissioned by the *North American Review,* describes the activities of emerging Negro institutions. Edward Roland Sill, a well-known poet and teacher at the University of California, submitted his essay on women's role in higher education as a letter to the editor of *Century Magazine.*

The collection is closed with an unsigned article dealing with the Chautauquan Institution. This remarkable organization, founded in 1874 and still active, had a significant impact on the American college and university. Through its Literary and Scientific Circle (C.L.S.C.) it clearly demonstrated a popular need for adult access to higher education. William R. Harper had played a major part in organizing correspondence study at Chautauqua and when he assumed the presidency of the new University of Chicago he incorporated a separate unit for university extension. Nationally, however, extension work languished and it was not until the first and second decades of the twentieth century that adult higher education took hold.

Section I

Academic Aspects

1

What Is a Liberal Education?

Charles W. Eliot

The general growth of knowledge and the rise of new literatures, arts, and sciences during the past two hundred and fifty years have made it necessary to define anew liberal education, and hence to enlarge the signification of the degree of bachelor of arts, which is the customary evidence of a liberal education. Already the meaning of this ancient degree has quietly undergone many serious modifications; it ought now to be fundamentally and openly changed.

The course of study which terminates in the degree of bachelor of arts ordinarily covers from seven to ten years, of which four are spent in college and three to six at school; and this long course is, for my present purpose, to be considered as a whole. I wish to demonstrate, first, that the number of school and college studies admissible with equal weight or rank for this highly valued degree needs to be much enlarged; secondly, that among admissible subjects a considerable range of choice should be allowed from an earlier age than that at which choice is now generally permitted; and, thirdly, that the existing order of studies should be changed in important respects. The phrase "studies admissible with equal weight or rank" requires some explanation. I use it to describe subjects which are taught with equal care and completeness, and are supported by the same

Reprinted from *Century Magazine*, Vol. 28, No. 2, June 1884, pp. 203-212.

prescriptions, and which win for their respective adherents equal admission to academic competitions, distinctions, and rewards, and equal access to the traditional goal of a liberal education, the degree of bachelor of arts. Coördinate studies must be on an equal footing in all respects: of two studies, if one is required and the other elective, if one is taught elaborately and fully and the other only in its elements, if honors and scholarships may be obtained through one and not through the other, if one may be counted toward the valuable degree of bachelor of arts and the other only toward the very inferior degree of bachelor of science or bachelor of philosophy, the two studies are not coördinate—they have not the same academic weight or rank.

The three principal propositions just enunciated lead to consequences which at first sight are repulsive to most men educated in the existing system. For example, it would follow from them that children might not receive the training which their fathers received; that young men educated simultaneously in the same institutions might not have knowledge of the same subjects, share precisely the same intellectual pleasures, or cultivate the same tastes; and that the degree of bachelor of arts would cease to indicate—what it has indicated for nearly three hundred years—that every recipient had devoted the larger part of his years of training to Latin, Greek, and mathematics. Proposals which lead to such results inevitably offend all minds naturally conservative. The common belief of most educated men in the indispensableness of the subjects in which they were themselves instructed, reënforces the general conservatism of mankind in regard to methods of education; and this useful conservatism is securely intrenched behind the general fact that anything which one generation is to impart to the next through educational institutions must, as a rule, be apprehended with tolerable precision by a considerable number of individuals of the elder generation. Hence, a new subject can only force its way very gradually into the circle of the arts called liberal. For instance, it was more than a hundred years after the widespread revival of Greek in Europe before that language was established at Paris and Oxford as a regular constituent in the academic curriculum; and physics and chemistry are not yet fully admitted to that curriculum, although Robert Boyle published his "New Experiments touching the Spring of the Air" in 1660, Galvani discovered animal electricity in 1790, Lavoisier analyzed water in 1783, and John Dalton published his "New System of Chemical Philosophy" in 1808. Indeed, so stout and insurmountable seem the barriers against progress in education, as we look forward, that we are rather startled on looking back to see how short a time what is has been.

It is the received opinion that mathematics is an indispensible and universal constituent of education, possessing the venerable sanction of immemorial use; but when we examine closely the matters now taught as mathematics in this country, we find that they are all recent inventions, of a character so distinct from the Greek geometry and conic sections which with arithmetic represented mathematics down to the seventeenth century, that they do not furnish the same mental training at all. As Whewell pointed out forty years ago, modern mathematics — algebra, analytic geometry, the differential and integral calculus, analytical mechanics, and quaternions — has almost put out of sight the ancient form of mathematical science. Leibnitz published his "Rules of the Differential Calculus" in 1684, Newton his "Method of Fluxions" in 1711, Euler his "Institutiones Calculi Integralis" in 1768-70; but Lagrange, Laplace, Monge, Legendre, Gauss, and Hamilton, the chief promulgators of what we now call mathematical science, all lived into or in this century. The name of this well-established constituent of the course of study required for the baccalaureate is old, but the thing itself is new. A brief citation from the conclusion of Whewell's prolix discussion of the educational value of mathematics, in his treatise entitled "Of a Liberal Education," will explain and fortify the statement that the mental discipline furnished by the mathematics of

Euclid and Archimedes was essentially different from that furnished by the analytical mathematics now almost exclusively in use:

> "On all these accounts, then, I venture to assert, that while we hold mathematics to be of inestimable value as a permanent study by which the reason of man is to be educated, we must hold also that the geometrical forms of mathematics must be especially preserved and maintained, as essentially requisite for this office; that analytical mathematics can in no way answer this purpose, and, if the attempt be made so to employ it, will not only be worthless, but highly prejudicial to men's minds."

The modern analytical mathematics, thus condemned by Whewell, is practically the only mathematics now in common use in the United States.

Again, it is obvious that the spirit and method in which Latin has been for the most part studied during the present century are very different from the spirit and method in which it was studied in the preceding centuries. During this century it has been taught as a dead language (except perhaps in parts of Italy and Hungary), whereas it used to be taught as a living language, the common speech of all scholars, both lay and clerical. Those advocates of classical learning who maintain that a dead language must have more disciplinary virtue than a living one, would hardly have been satisfied with the prevailing modes of teaching and learning Latin in any century before our own. At any rate, it was a different discipline which Latin supplied when young scholars learned not only to read it, but to write and speak it with fluency.

I venture to inquire next how long Greek has held its present place in the accepted scheme of liberal education. Although the study of Greek took root in Italy as early as 1400, and was rapidly diffused there after the fall of Constantinople in 1453, it can hardly be said to have become established at Paris as a subject worthy the attention of scholars before 1458, or at Oxford before the end of the fifteenth century. At Paris, for many years after 1458, Greek was taught with indifferent success, and its professors, who were mostly foreigners, were excluded from the privileges of regency in the University. In-

deed, the subject seems to have long been in the condition of
what we should now call an extra study, and its teachers were
much in the position of modern-language teachers in an American college, which does not admit them to the faculty. Grocyn,
Linacre, and Latimer, who learned Greek at Florence, introduced the study at Oxford in the last years of the fifteenth
century; but Anthony Wood says that Grocyn gave lectures
of his own free will, and without any emolument. It is certain
that in 1578 the instruction in Greek which was given to under-
graduates at Cambridge started with the elements of the language; and it is altogether probable that Greek had no real
hold in the English grammar schools until the end of the sixteenth century. The statutes which were adopted by the University of Paris in the year 1600 define the studies in arts to
be Latin, Greek, Aristotle's philosophy, and Euclid; and they
make Greek one of the requirements for admission to the
School of Law. It took two hundred years, then, for the Greek
language and literature gradually to displace in great part the
scholastic metaphysics which, with scholastic theology, had
been for generations regarded as the main staple of liberal
education; and this displacement was accomplished only after
the same sort of tedious struggle by which the new knowledges
of the eighteenth and nineteenth centuries are now winning
their way to academic recognition. The revived classical
literature was vigorously and sincerely opposed as frivolous,
heterodox, and useless for discipline; just as natural history,
chemistry, physics, and modern literatures are now opposed.
The conservatives of that day used precisely the same argu-
ments which the conservatives of to-day bring forward, only
they were used against classical literature then, while now they
are used in its support. Let it not be imagined that the scholastic metaphysics and theology, which lost most of the ground
won by Greek, were in the eyes of the educated men of the
twelfth to the sixteenth century at all what they seem to us.
They were the chief delight of the wise, learned, and pious;
they were the best mental food of at least twelve generations;
and they aroused in Europe an enthusiasm for study which has

hardly been equaled in later centuries. When Abélard taught at Paris early in the twelfth century, thousands of pupils flocked around his chair; when the Dominican Thomas Aquinas wrote his "Summa Theologiae," and lectured at Paris, Bologna, Rome, and Naples, in the middle of the thirteenth century, he had a prodigious following, and for three centuries his fame and influence grew; when the Franciscan Duns Scotus lectured at Oxford at the beginning of the fourteenth century, the resort of students to the university seems to have been far greater than it has ever been since. We may be sure that these wonders were not wrought with dust or chaff. Nevertheless, the scholastic theology and metaphysics were in large measure displaced, and for three hundred years the classical literatures have reigned in their stead.

Authentic history records an earlier change of a fundamental sort in the list of arts called liberal, and consequently in the recognized scheme of liberal education. When Erasmus was a student, that is, in the last third of the fifteenth century, before Greek had been admitted to the circle of the liberal arts, the regular twelve years' course of study included, and had long included, reading, arithmetic, grammar, syntax, poetry, rhetoric, metaphysics, and theology, all studied in Latin; and of these subjects metaphysics and theology occupied half of the whole time, and all of the university period. But in the eleventh century, before Abélard founded scholastic theology, the authoritative list of liberal studies was quite different. It was given in the single line:

"Lingua, tropus, ratio, numerus, tonus, angulus, astra."

Most students were content with the first three — grammar, rhetoric, and logic; a few also pursued arithmetic, music, geometry, and astronomy, if these grave names may be properly applied to the strange mixtures of fact and fancy which in obscure Latin versions of Greek and Arabian originals passed for science. It was this privileged circle which scholastic divinity successfully invaded at the beginning of the twelfth century, the success of the invasion being probably due to the fact that religion was then the only thing which could be systematically studied.

This hasty retrospect shows, first, that some of the studies now commonly called liberal have not long held their present preëminence; and, secondly, that new learning has repeatedly forced its way, in times past, to full academic standing, in spite of the opposition of the conservative, and of the keener resistance of established teachers and learned bodies, whose standing is always supposed to be threatened by the rise of new sciences. History teaches boldness in urging the claims of modern literatures and sciences to full recognition as liberal arts.

The first subject which, as I conceive, is entitled to recognition as of equal academic value or rank with any subject now most honored is the English language and literature. When Greek began to revive in Europe, English was just acquiring a literary form; but when Greek had won its present rank among the liberal arts, Shakspere had risen, the English language was formed, and English literature was soon to become the greatest of modern literatures. How does it stand now, with its immense array of poets, philosophers, historians, commentators, critics, satirists, dramatists, novelists, and orators? It cannot be doubted that English literature is beyond all comparison the amplest, most various, and most splendid literature which the world has seen; and it is enough to say of the English language that it is the language of that literature. Greek literature compares with English as Homer compares with Shakspere, that is, as infantile with adult civilization. It may further be said of the English language that it is the native tongue of nations which are preëminent in the world by force of character, enterprise, and wealth, and whose political and social institutions have a higher moral interest and greater promise than any which mankind has hitherto invented. To the original creations of English genius are to be added translations into Engligh of all the masterpieces of other literatures, sacred and profane. It is a very rare scholar who has not

29

learned much more about the Jews, the Greeks, or the Romans through English than through Hebrew, Greek, or Latin.

And now, with all this wonderful treasure within reach of our youth, what is the position of American schools and colleges in regard to teaching English? Has English literature the foremost place in the programmes of schools? By no means; at best only a subordinate place, and in many schools no place at all. Does English take equal rank with Greek or Latin in our colleges? By no means; not in the number and rank of the teachers, nor in the consideration in which the subject is held by faculty and students, nor in the time which may be devoted to it by a candidate for a degree. Until within a few years the American colleges made no demand upon candidates for admission in regard to knowledge of English; and now that some colleges make a small requirement in English, the chief result of the examinations is to demonstrate the woful ignorance of their own language and literature which prevails among the picked youth of the country. Shall we be told, as usual, that the best way to learn English is to study Latin and Greek? The answer is, that the facts do not corroborate this improbable hypothesis. American youth in large numbers study Latin and Greek, but do not thereby learn English. Moreover, this hypothesis is obviously inapplicable to the literatures. Shall we also be told, as usual, that no linguistic discipline can be got out of the study of the native language? How, then, was the Greek mind trained in language? Shall we be told that knowledge of English literature should be picked up without systematic effort? The answer is, first, that as a matter of fact this knowledge is not picked up by American youth; and, secondly, that there never was any good reason to suppose that it would be, the acquisition of a competent knowledge of English literature being not an easy but a laborious undertaking for an average youth – not a matter of entertaining reading, but of serious study. Indeed, there is no subject in which competent guidance and systematic instruction are of greater value. For ten years past Harvard University has been trying, first, to stimulate the preparatory schools to give

30

attention to English, and, secondly, to develop and improve its own instruction in that department; but its success has thus far been very moderate. So little attention is paid to English at the preparatory schools that half of the time, labor, and money which the University spends upon English must be devoted to the mere elements of the subject. Moreover, this very year at Harvard less than half as much instruction, of proper university grade, is offered in English as in Greek or in Latin. The experience of all other colleges and universities resembles in this respect that of Harvard.

This comparative neglect of the greatest of literatures in American schools and colleges is certainly a remarkable phenomenon. How is it to be explained? First, by the relative newness of this language and literature: it requires two or three hundred years to introduce new intellectual staples; secondly, by the real difficulty of teaching English well — a difficulty which has only of late years been overcome; and, thirdly, by the dazzling splendor of the revived Greek and Latin literatures when in the fourteenth and fifteenth centuries they broke upon the mind of Western Europe. Through the force of custom, tradition, inherited tastes, and transmitted opinions, the educational practices of to-day are still cast in the molds of the seventeenth century. The scholars of that time saw a great light which shone out of darkness, and they worshiped it; and we, their descendants in the ninth generation, upon whom greater lights have arisen, still worship at the same shrine. Let us continue to worship there; but let us pay at least equal honors to the glorious lights which have since been kindled.

The next subjects for which I claim a position of academic equality with Greek, Latin, and mathematics are French and German. This claim rests not on the usefulness of these languages to couriers, tourists, or commercial travelers, and not on their merit as languages, but on the magnitude and worth of the literatures, and on the unquestionable fact that facility in reading these languages is absolutely indispensable to a scholar, whatever may be his department of study. Until

31

within one hundred or one hundred and fifty years, scholarship had a common language, the Latin; so that scholars of all the European nationalities had a perfect means of communication, whether in speaking, writing, or printing. But the cultivation of the spirit of nationality and the development of national literatures have brought about the abandonment of Latin as the common language of learning, and imposed on every student who would go beyond the elements of his subject the necessity of acquiring at least a reading knowledge of French and German, besides Latin. Indeed, the advanced student of our day can dispense with Latin better than with French, German, or English; for, although the antiquated publications in any science may be printed in Latin, the recent (which will probably contain all that is best in the old) will be found printed in one of these modern languages.

I cannot state too strongly the indispensableness of both French and German to the American or English student. Without these languages he will be much worse off in respect to communicating with his contemporaries than was the student of the seventeenth century who could read and speak Latin; for through Latin the student of the year 1684 could put himself into direct communication with all contemporary learning. So far as I know, there is no difference of opinion among American scholars as to the need of mastering these two languages in youth. The philologists, archaeologists, metaphysicians, physicians, physicists, naturalists, chemists, economists, engineers, architects, artists, and musicians, all agree that a knowledge of these languages is indispensable to the intelligent pursuit of any one of their respective subjects beyond its elements. Every college professor who gives a thorough course of instruction—no matter in what department—finds himself obliged to refer his pupils to French and German authorities. In the reference library of any modern laboratory, whether of chemistry, physics, physiology, pathology, botany, or zoology, a large proportion of the books will be found to be in French or German. The working library of the philologist, archaeologist, or historian teaches the same lesson. Without a knowledge of these two languages it is impossible to get at the experience of the world upon any modern industrial, social, or financial question, or to master any profession which depends upon applications of modern science. I urge no utilitarian argument, but rest the claims of French and German for admission to complete academic equality on the copiousness and merit of the literatures, and the indispensableness of the languages to all scholars.

Such being the reasons for teaching French and German to all young scholars at an early stage of their training, what is the condition of these languages at American schools and colleges? For answer to this question I will describe the condition of instruction in French and German at Yale College, an institution, I need not say, which holds a leading position among American colleges. No knowledge of either French or German is required for admission to Yale College, and no instruction is provided in either language before the beginning of the Junior year. In that year German must be and French may be studied, each four hours a week; in the Senior year either language may be studied four hours a week. In other words, Yale College does not suggest that the preparatory schools ought to teach either French or German, does not give its students the opportunity of acquiring these languages in season to use them in other studies, and does not offer them any adequate opportunity of becoming acquainted with the literature of either language before they take the bachelor's degree. Could we have stronger evidence than this of the degraded condition of French and German in the mass of our schools and colleges? A few colleges have lately been demanding a small amount of French or German for admission, and a few schools have met this very moderate demand; but, as a general rule, American boys who go to college devote from two to three solid years to Greek and Latin, but study French and German scarcely at all while at school, and at college only for a part of the time during the later half of the course. The opportunities and facilities for studying Greek and Latin in our schools and colleges are none too great; but surely the opportunities and facilities for

33

studying French and German are far too small. The modern
languages should be put on an equality with the ancient.

The next subject which demands an entirely different position from that it now occupies in American schools and colleges is history. If any study is liberal and liberalizing, it is
the modern study of history — the study of the passions, opinions, beliefs, arts, laws, and institutions of different races or
communities, and of the joys, sufferings, conflicts, and achievements of mankind. Philology and polite literature arrogate the
title of the "humanities"; but what study can so justly claim
that honorable title as the study which deals with the actual
experience on this earth of social and progressive man? What
kind of knowledge can be so useful to a legislator, admin-
istrator, journalist, publicist, philanthropist, or philosopher as
a well-ordered knowledge of history? If the humanity or liberality of a study depends upon its power to enlarge the intellectual and moral interests of the student, quicken his
sympathies, impel him to the side of truth and virtue, and make
him loathe falsehood and vice, no study can be more humane
or liberal than history. These being the just claims of history
in general, the history of the community and nation to which
we belong has a still more pressing claim upon our attention.
That study shows the young the springs of public honor and
dishonor; sets before them the national failings, weaknesses,
and sins; warns them against future dangers by exhibiting the
losses and sufferings of the past; enshrines in their hearts
the national heroes; and strengthens in them the precious love
of country. One would naturally suppose that the history of
the United States and England, at least, would hold an important place in the programmes of American schools and colleges, and that no subject would occupy a more dignified position in the best colleges and universities than history in respect to the number and rank of its teachers. The facts do not
accord with this natural supposition. The great majority of
American colleges (there are nearly four hundred of them)
make no requirements in history for admission, and have no
teacher of history whatever. Lest it be imagined that this

can be true only of inferior colleges, I will mention that
in so old and well-established a college as Dartmouth there
is no teacher of history, whether professor, tutor, or temporary instructor; while in so excellent an institution as
Princeton there is only one professor of history against three
of Greek, and this single professor includes political science
with history in his teaching. No institution which calls itself
a college expects to do without a professor of Greek, or of
Latin, or of mathematics; but nearly all of them do without
a teacher of history. The example of the colleges governs
the preparatory schools. When young men who are interested
in historical study ask me if it would be advisable for them to
fit themselves to teach history for a livelihood, I am obliged
to say that it would be the height of imprudence on their part,
there being only an infinitesimal demand for competent teachers of history in our whole country. This humiliated condition
of history is only made the more conspicuous by the old practice, which still obtains at some colleges (Harvard College,
for instance), of demanding from all candidates for admission
a small amount of Greek and Roman history—as much as a
clever boy could commit to memory in three or four days. One
hardly knows which most to wonder at in this requirement,
the selection of topic or the minuteness of the amount. Is it
not plain that the great subject of history holds no proper
place in American education?

Closely allied to the study of history is the study of the new
science called political economy, or public economics. I say
the new science, because Smith's "Wealth of Nations" was
not published until 1776; Malthus's "Essay on the Principle
of Population" only appeared in 1798; and Ricardo's "Political Economy and Taxation," in 1817. The subject is
related to history inasmuch as it gleans its most important
facts by the study of the institutions and industrial and social
conditions of the past; it is the science of wealth in so far
as it deals with the methods by which private or national
wealth is accumulated, protected, enjoyed, bnd distributed;
and it is connected with ethics in that it deals with social

35

theories and the moral effects of economic conditions. In some of its aspects it were better called the science of the health of nations; for its results show how nations might happily grow and live in conformity with physical and moral laws. It is by far the most complex and difficult of the sciences of which modern education has to take account, and therefore should not be introduced too early into the course of study for the degree of bachelor of arts; but when it is introduced, enough of it should be offered to the student to enable him to get more than a smattering.

When we consider how formidable are the industrial, social, and political problems with which the next generations must grapple, — when we observe how inequalities of condition increase, notwithstanding the general acceptance of theories of equality; how population irresistibly tends to huge agglomerations in spite of demonstrations that such agglomerations are physically and morally unhealthy; how the universal thirst for the enjoyments of life grows hotter and hotter and is not assuaged; how the relations of government to society become constantly more and more complicated, while the governing capacity of men does not seem to increase proportionally; and how free institutions commit to masses of men the determination of public policy in regard to economic problems of immense difficulty, such as the problems concerning tariffs, banking, currency, the domestic carrying trade, foreign commerce, and the incidence of taxes, — we can hardly fail to appreciate the importance of offering to large numbers of American students ample facilities for learning all that is known of economic science.

How does the ordinary provision made in our colleges for the study of political economy meet this need of students and of the community? That I may not understate this provision, I will describe the provisions made at Columbia College, an institution which is said to be the richest of our colleges, and at Brown University, one of the most substantial of the New England colleges. At Columbia, Juniors must attend two exercises a week in political economy for half the year, and Seniors may elect that subject for two hours a week throughout the year. At Brown, Juniors may elect political economy two hours a week for half the year, and Seniors have a like privilege. The provision of instruction in Greek at Brown is five and a half times as much as the provision in political economy, and seven-elevenths of the Greek is required of all students, besides the Greek which was required at school; but none of the political economy is required. Columbia College makes a further provision of instruction in history, law, and political science for students who are able to devote either one or two years to these subjects after taking the degree of bachelor of arts, or who are willing to procure one year's instruction in these subjects by accepting the degree of bachelor of philosophy instead of the degree of bachelor of arts— a very high price to pay for this one year's privilege. If this is the state of things in two leading Eastern colleges with regard to instruction in political economy, what should we find to be the average provision in American colleges? We should find it poor in quality and insignificant in amount. In view of this comparative neglect of a subject all-important to our own generation and those which are to follow, one is tempted to join in the impatient cry, Are our young men being educated for the work of the twentieth century or of the seventeenth? There can be no pretense that political economy is an easy subject, or that it affords no mental discipline. Indeed, it requires such exactness of statement, such accurate weighing of premises, and such closeness of reasoning, that many young men of twenty, who have been disciplined by the study of Greek, Latin, and mathematics for six or eight years, find that it tasks their utmost powers. Neither can it be justly called a material or utilitarian subject; for it is full of grave moral problems, and deals with many questions of public honor and duty.

The last subject for which I claim admission to the magic circle of the liberal arts is natural science. All the subjects which the sixteenth century decided were liberal, and all the subjects which I have heretofore discussed, are studied in books; but natural science is to be studied not in books but

37

in things. The student of languages, letters, philosophy, mathematics, history, or political economy, reads books, or listens to the words of his teacher. The student of natural science scrutinizes, touches, weighs, measures, analyzes, dissects, and watches things. By these exercises his powers of observation and judgment are trained, and he acquires the precious habit of observing the appearances, transformations, and processes of nature. Like the hunter and the artist, he has open eyes and an educated judgment in seeing. He is at home in some large tract of nature's domain. Finally, he acquires the scientific method of study in the field, where that method was originally perfected. In our day, the spirit in which a true scholar will study Indian arrowheads, cuneiform inscriptions, or reptile tracks in sandstone, is one and the same, although these objects belong respectively to three separate sciences — archaeology, philology, and palaeontology. But what is this spirit? It is the patient, cautious, sincere, self-directing spirit of natural science. One of the best of living classical scholars, Professor Jebb of Glasgow, states this fact in the following forcible words: "The diffusion of that which is specially named science has at the same time spread abroad the only spirit in which any kind of knowledge can be prosecuted to a result of lasting intellectual value." Again, the arts built upon chemistry, physics, botany, zoology, and geology are chief factors in the civilization of our time, and are growing in material and moral influence at a marvelous rate. Since the beginning of this century, they have wrought wonderful changes in the physical relation of man to the earth which he inhabits, in national demarkations, in industrial organization, in governmental functions, and in the modes of domestic life; and they will certainly do as much for the twentieth century as they have done for ours. They are not simply mechanical or material forces; they are also moral forces of great intensity. I maintain that the young science which has already given to all sciences a new and better spirit and method, and to civilization new powers and resources of infinite range, deserves to be admitted with all possible honors to the circle of the liberal arts; and that a study fitted to train noble faculties, which are not trained by the studies now chiefly pursued in youth, ought to be admitted on terms of perfect equality to the academic curriculum.

The wise men of the fifteenth century took the best intellectual and moral materials existing in their day, — namely, the classical literatures, metaphysics, mathematics, and systematic theology, — and made of them the substance of the education which they called liberal. When we take the best intellectual and moral materials of their day and of ours to make up the list of subjects worthy to rank as liberal, and to be studied for discipline, ought we to omit that natural science which in its outcome supplies some of the most important forces of modern civilization? We do omit it. I do not know a single preparatory school in this country in which natural science has an adequate place, or any approach to an adequate place, although some beginnings have lately been made. There is very little profit in studying natural science in a book, as if it were grammar or history; for nothing of the peculiar discipline which the proper study of science supplies can be obtained in that way, although some information on scientific subjects may be so acquired. In most colleges a little scientific information is offered to the student through lectures and the use of manuals, but no scientific training. The science is rarely introduced as early as the Sophomore year; generally it begins only with the Junior year, by which time the mind of the student has become so set in the habits which the study of languages and mathematics engenders, that he finds great difficulty in grasping the scientific method. It seems to him absurd to perform experiments or make dissections. Can he not read in a book, or see in a picture, what the results will be? The only way to prevent this disproportionate development of the young mind on the side of linguistic and abstract reasoning, is to introduce into school courses of study a fair amount of training in sciences of observation. Over against four languages, the elements of mathematics, and the elements of history, there must be set some accurate study of things. Were other argument needed, I should find it in the great addition to the enjoyment of life which results from an early acquaintance and constant intimacy with the wonders and beauties of external nature. For boy and man this intimacy is a source of ever fresh delight.

To the list of studies which the sixteenth century called liberal, I would therefore add, as studies of equal rank, English, French, German, history, political economy, and natural science, not one of which can be said to have existed in mature form when the definition of liberal education, which is still in force, was laid down. In a large university many other languages and sciences will be objects of study; I confine myself here to those studies which, in my judgment, are most desirable in an ordinary college. We are now in position to consider how the necessity for allowing choice among studies has arisen.

The second and third of the three principal propositions which I wish to demonstrate—namely, that earlier choice should be allowed among coördinate studies, and that the existing order of studies needs to be modified—may be treated much more briefly than the first proposition, although in them lies the practical application of the whole discussion. When the men of the sixteenth century had taken all the sciences known to their generation to make up their curriculum of liberal study, the sum was not so large as to make it impossible for a student to cover the whole ground effectually. But if the list of liberal arts is extended, as I have urged, it is manifest that no man can cover the whole ground and get a thorough knowledge of any subject. Hence the necessity of allowing the student to choose among many coördinate studies the few to which he will devote himself. In a vain endeavor to introduce at least some notions about the new sciences into the curriculum of the year 1600, the managers of American colleges have made it impossible for the student to get a thorough knowledge of any subject whatever. The student has a better chance to learn Greek and Latin than anything else; but he does not get instruction enough in these languages to enable him to master them. In no other subject can he possibly get beyond the elements, if he keep within the official schedules of studies. Consider what sort of an idea of metaphysics can be obtained from a single text-book of moderate size, into which the whole vast subject has been filtered through one preoccupied mind; or of physics from a short course of lectures and a little manual of three or four hundred pages prepared by a teacher who is not himself an investigator; or of political economy from a single short treatise by an author not of the first rank. These are not imaginary sketches; they are described from the life. Such are the modes of dealing with these sciences which prevail in the great majority of American colleges. I need not dwell upon this great evil, which is doing untold injury every year. The remedies are plain. First, let the new studies be put in every respect on a level with the old; and then let such a choice among coördinate studies be given as to secure to the student a chance to be thorough in something. To be effective, option must be permitted earlier than it is now. This proposition—that earlier options are desirable—cannot be discussed without simultaneously considering the order of studies at school and college.

Boyhood is the best time to learn new languages; so that as many as possible of the four languages, French, German, Latin, and Greek, ought to be begun at school. But if all boys who are to receive a liberal education are required to learn to read all four languages before they go to college, those boys who are not quick at languages will have very little time for other studies. English, the elements of mathematics, the elements of some natural science properly taught, and the history of England and the United States being assumed as fundamentals, it is evident that some choice among the four remaining languages must be allowed, in order not to unduly restrict the number of boys who go to college. With very good instruction, many boys could doubtless learn to read all four languages tolerably well before they were eighteen years old without sacrificing more essential things; but there are boys of excellent capacity in other subjects who could not accomplish this linguistic task; and in many States of the Union it is quite impossible to get very good instruction in all these

41

languages. Therefore I believe that an option should be allowed among these four languages at college admission examinations, any three being accepted, and the choice being determined in each case by the wishes of parents, the advice of teachers, the destination of the candidate if settled, the better quality of accessible instruction in one language than in another, or the convenience of the school which the candidate attends. Whichever language the candidate did not offer at admission he should have opportunity to begin and pursue at college.

As to the best order in which to take up these four languages, I notice that most persons who have thought of the matter hold some theory about it with more or less confidence, but that the English-speaking peoples have little or no experience upon the subject. One would naturally suppose that easiest first, hardest last, would be a good rule; but such is not the present practice in this country. On the contrary, Latin is often begun before French; and it is common to begin Greek at fourteen and German at twenty. In education, as in other things, I am a firm believer in the principle of expending the least force which will accomplish the object in view. If a language is to be learned, I would teach it in the easiest known method, and at the age when it can be easiest learned. But there is another theory which is often acted upon, though seldom explicitly stated, — the theory that, for the sake of discipline, hardness that is avoidable should be deliberately imposed upon boys; as, for instance, by forcing a boy to study many languages, who has no gifts that way, and can never attain to any mastery of them. To my mind the only justification of any kind of discipline, training, or drill is attainment of the appropriate end of that discipline. It is a waste for society, and an outrage upon the individual, to make a boy spend the years when he is most teachable in a discipline, the end of which he can never reach, when he might have spent them in a different discipline, which would have been rewarded by achievement. Herein lies the fundamental reason for options among school as well as college studies, all of which are liberal.

42

A mental discipline which takes no account of differences of capacity and taste is not well directed. It follows that there must be variety in education instead of uniform prescription. To ignorant or thoughtless people it seems that the wisdom and experience of the world ought to have produced by this time a uniform course of instruction good for all boys, and made up of studies permanently preëminent; but there are two strong reasons for believing that this convenient result is unattainable: in the first place, the uniform boy is lacking; and in the second place, it is altogether probable that the educational value of any established study, far from being permanently fixed, is constantly changing as new knowledge accumulates and new sciences come into being. Doubtless the eleventh century thought it had a permanent curriculum in *"Lingua, tropus, ratio, numerus, tonus, angulus, astra";* doubtless the course of study which Erasmus followed was held by the teachers of that day to supply the only sufficient liberal education; and we all know that since the year 1600, or thereabouts, it has been held by the wisest and most cultivated men that Greek, Latin, and mathematics are the only good disciplinary studies. Whewell, whose foible was omniscience, did not hesitate to apply to these three studies the word *permanent*. But if history proves that the staples of education have in fact changed, reason says still more clearly that they must change. It would be indeed incredible that organized education should not take account of the progress of knowledge. We may be sure that the controlling intellectual forces of the actual world, century by century, penetrate educational processes, and that languages, literatures, philosophies, or sciences which show themselves fruitful and powerful must win recognition as liberal arts and proper means of mental discipline.

Two objections to the views which I have been presenting occur at once to every conservative mind. I have often been met with the question: Is this traditional degree of bachelor of arts, which for three hundred years, at least, has had a tolerably clear meaning, to be deprived of all exact significance, so that it will be impossible to tell what one who holds the degree has studied? I reply that the degree will continue to testify to the main fact to which it now bears witness, namely, that the recipient has spent eight or ten years, somewhere between the ages of twelve and twenty-three, in liberal studies. I might add that the most significant and valuable degree in arts which is anywhere given—the German degree of doctor of philosophy and master of arts—does not stand for any particular studies, and does not indicate in any individual case the special studies for which it was conferred, although it does presuppose the earlier accomplishment, at a distance of several years, of the curriculum of a German gymnasium.

A second objection is expressed in the significant question: What will become of Greek and Latin if all these new subjects are put on an equality with them? Will Greek and Latin, and the culture which they represent, survive the invasion? To this question I answer, first, that it is proposed, not to substitute new subjects for the old, but only to put new subjects beside the old in a fair competition, and not to close any existing road to the degree of bachelor of arts, but only to open new ones; secondly, that the proposed modification of the present prescription of Greek and Latin for all boys who are to go to college will rid the Greek and Latin classes of unwilling and incapable pupils, to the great advantage of the pupils who remain; and, thirdly, that the withdrawal of the artificial protection now given to the classics will cause the study of classical antiquity to rely—to use the well-chosen words of Professor Jebb on the last page of his life of Bentley—"no longer upon a narrow or exclusive prescription, but upon a reasonable perception of its proper place amongst the studies which belong to a liberal education." The higher the value which one sets on Greek and Latin as means of culture, the firmer must be his belief in the permanence of those studies when they cease to be artificially protected. In education, as elsewhere, it is the fittest that survives. The classics, like other studies, must stand upon their own merits; for it is not the proper business of universities to force subjects of study, or particular kinds of mental discipline, upon unwilling generations; and they cannot prudently undertake that function, especially in a country where they have no support from an established church, or from an aristocratic organization of society, and where it would be so easy for the generations, if repelled, to pass the universities by.

Finally, the enlargement of the circle of liberal arts may justly be urged on the ground that the interests of the higher education and of the institutions which supply that education demand it. Liberal education is not safe and strong in a country in which the great majority of the men who belong to the intellectual professions are not liberally educated. Now, that is just the case in this country. The great majority of the men who are engaged in the practice of law and medicine, in journalism, the public service, and the scientific professions, and in industrial leadership, are not bachelors of arts. Indeed, the only learned profession which contains to-day a large proportion of bachelors of arts is the ministry. This sorry condition of things is doubtless due in part to what may be called the pioneer condition of American society; but I think it is also due to the antiquated state of the common college curriculum, and of the course of preparatory study at school. When institutions of learning cut themselves off from the sympathy and support of large numbers of men whose lives are intellectual, by refusing to recognize as liberal arts and disciplinary studies languages, literatures, and sciences which seem to these men as important as any which the institutions cultivate, they inflict a gratuitous injury both on themselves and on the country which they should serve. Their refusal to listen to parents and teachers who ask that the avenues of approach to them may be increased in number, the new roads rising to the same grade or level as the old, would be an indication that a gulf already yawned between them and large bodies of men who by force of character, intelligence, and practical training are very influential in the modern world. For twenty years past signs have not been wanting that the American college was not keeping pace with the growth of the country in population and wealth. I believe that a chief cause of this relative decline is the narrowness of the course of study in both school and college.

The execution of the principles which I have advocated would involve considerable changes in the order of school and college studies. Thus, science-teaching should begin early in the school course; English should be studied from the beginning of school life to the end of college life; and the order in which the other languages are taken up should be for many boys essentially changed. We should in vain expect such changes to be made suddenly. They must be gradually brought about by the pressure of public opinion — by the public opinion of the educated classes taking gradual effect through established educational instrumentalities. The change will be wrought by the demands of parents upon private schools; by the influence of trustees and committees in charge of endowed and public schools upon school courses of study; by the conditions which benefactors and founders impose upon their gifts and bequests to liberal education; by the competition of industrial and technological schools; and by the gradual encroachment of the modern subjects upon the ancient in colleges and universities. All these influences are at work, and much ground has been gained during the last fifteen years.

2

Must the Classics Go?

Andrew F. West

Is classical training necessary in liberal education? To appreciate this question we must first know what education means.
Every man is born into this world ignorant both of himself
and his surroundings, but to act his part so as to reach success
and happiness needs to understand them both. Therefore, he
must learn; and having to learn, must be educated. This will
involve two processes:

1. The development of man's power to master himself and
circumstances, by training every capacity to its highest energy,
—discipline. 2. Communication of the most valuable knowledge, —information. Both are necessary. Discipline precedes
information, because power precedes acquisition. Information
completes discipline by yielding actual results in the world. In
a word, discipline gives power to acquire information, and the
total result is culture.

The two great instruments of educational discipline and
information have hitherto been mathematics and language,
leading to physical, intellectual, and social sciences, and these
again culminating in a philosophy or study of first principles
of all things. On this basis our college education has been
built. None propose excluding mathematics. Few question the

Reprinted from *North American Review,* Vol. 138, No. 327, Feb.
1884, pp. 151-162.

need of studying language in some form. But when the classical languages are proposed as essential to liberal education, objections arise and pronounced attacks are made. I propose merely three things:

I. To enumerate the objectors and answer their objections.

II. To state the positive argument for classical training.

III. To state the reasons for retaining Greek as well as Latin.

I. The objectors and their objections. These are:

1. Men of active rather than contemplative temperament. They care chiefly for what prepares immediately for some specific calling, and are so absorbed in civil and commercial activities that they value only what bears obviously in these lines. John Stuart Mill has well shown the weakness of this position:

"Experience proves that there is no one study or pursuit which, practiced to the exclusion of all others, does not narrow and pervert the mind; breeding in it a class of prejudices special to that pursuit, besides a general prejudice common to all narrow specialities against large views from an incapacity to take in and appreciate the grounds of them. We need to know more than the one thing that is to be our principal occupation. This should be known as well as it can be known, but we should also acquire a clear general knowledge of the leading truths of all the great subjects of human interest."

2. Those who have never studied the classics. Many are college graduates. But their objection, if good, is good against any study they may have failed to appreciate from want of proper teaching, of application, or of capacity. Herbert Spencer, a pronounced enemy of the classics, does not profess to read them except in translations. In this respect, many college men resemble Mr. Spencer.

3. Those who are imbued with the money-making spirit of the age. These, if they believed that studying Greek and Latin was the road to wealth, would all worship classical culture. But to-day the obvious, the "effective," the "realistic," the perversely vulgar, nursed on money-worship and covered skin-deep with affected cultivation, is too apt to crowd out

the thoughtful and refined, and smother to death the heroic. Neither the hostility nor the approbation of this element counts for anything, because wholly ignorant and selfish.

4. Those who dislike classical studies because of distaste for any severe training, and a corresponding relish for lighter arts and accomplishments. They want culture only so far as it is immediately enjoyable. They desire results without the process, and so would resist thorough training in anything. Hence they answer themselves.

5. Those who believe literature necessary, but think modern languages should be substituted, as being genuine literature, and a necessary part of modern life. But to study modern languages we do not need to displace the classics. The trouble here is not the difficulty of making place for an extensive language course, but the prevalence of bungling methods of teaching, and the excessive time wasted on elementary mathematics, especially arithmetic, in so many schools. No such trouble exists in Germany. There, only one-sixth of the time, at the most, goes to mathematics, while to language even the Realschulen, or scientific schools, give two-sixths, and the Gymnasia four-sixths of their time. If, then, there is room for both, why not teach both? Suppose, however, we have to make the choice. The reasons for retaining the classics would be most cogent.

First. Because they are immeasurably superior to modern languages as means of discipline. Their structure is regular and highly complex. Modern languages do not contain material out of which to construct a logical grammar like theirs. What does English, French, or German grammar amount to? Simply *débris* of the classical languages, mixed with barbaric elements.

Second. Even if modern languages equaled the classics in structure, they would be less likely to be used consistently for discipline. So much time necessarily goes to mastering pronunciation and acquiring merely facility of use, which necessitates only inferior mental effort, that this is often mistaken for mastery of the language. Furthermore, modern languages are too near our own modes of thinking to help us enlarge our

49

knowledge in kind by entering widely different fields of thought, as we need to do.

Third. No modern languages have yet stood the great test of permanence which the classics have now endured for more then twenty centuries. Only a dozen generations have read Shakespeare. But Homer has already led the way to literary immortality for a hundred generations, with Plato, Virgil, and Horace not far behind.

Fourth. Modern languages, just because modern, are growing, and hence ever changing. This unfits them to be a permanent basis for culture.

6. Some advocates of physical science. Their objection is that science (meaning physical science) furnishes better discipline and information than the classics or anything else. Suppose it does. Must we study only physical science? Is there no room for any other training? May not classical training be scientific too? If correct, must it not be scientific?

But this objection is composite. Let us examine its parts; they are as clearly stated in Herbert Spencer's book, "Education," as anywhere.

"But now mark that, while for the training of mere memory, science is as good as, if not better than, language, it has an immense superiority in the kind of memory it cultivates . . . . Language establishes 'connections of ideas' based upon facts 'in a great measure accidental,' but science upon facts 'mostly necessary.' Though words and their meanings have relations 'in some sense natural'; yet since 'in the acquisition of languages as ordinarily carried on, these natural relations between words and their meanings are not habitually traced nor the laws regulating them explained, it must be admitted that they are commonly learned as fortuitous relations. On the other hand, the relations presented by science are causal relations, and, when properly taught, are understood as such.' Language 'exercises memory only, the other exercises both memory and understanding.' "

What greater error could be written? Examine it: science is superior in "the kind of memory it cultivates," — that is, causal memory. Is there no causal memory in learning the structure of the Greek verb, the "build" of complex etymology, the

50

orderly logic of syntax? Can it avoid being causal? Are there not laws of discourse, necessities in order and display of thought? Is antique civilization—the one world-wide civilization of history, all whose features are in its literature, whose rise, organic growth, decay, and death, run in long lines for centuries, to be learned by rote?

But Mr. Spencer's contrast is made out in unfair language. It is not allowable to draw inferences, as if from premises of equal value, by phrasing things in this way, "the acquisition of languages, as ordinarily carried on," and then, "the relations which science presents are casual relations, and, when properly taught, are understood as such." Of course they are, and so are they in language, "when properly taught." His next objection—that science better cultivates the judgment—is of the same nature as his remarks on memory. He fails to see that classical study deals not merely with words, but with things, with a vast body of remarkable fundamental phenomena, and hence the judgment must be highly exercised.

Mr. Spencer next insists that science is best for moral training.

"The learning of languages tends, if anything, to increase the already undue respect for authority .... By the pupil, the teacher's or grammar's dicta are received as unquestionable. His constant attitude of mind is that of submission to dogmatic teaching. And a necessary result is to accept without inquiry whatever is established. Quite opposite is the frank, independent attitude of mind generated by the cultivation of science."

This is simple quibbling. Apply it to any science, say chemistry, and you could not require a student to "submit" to the "dogmatic teaching" that inculcates authoritatively (though only provisionally) its symbols, atomic weights, formulae, specific gravities, and entire stock-knowledge. So in history, in teaching events and dates. So in arithmetic, numbers and their relations must first be learned arbitrarily or not learned at all. So in teaching a child the alphabet or even his own name.

But this is self-destructive also, as already hinted. All teaching must be instilled dogmatically at first, and, unless the pupil

51

accepts it, no progress of any sort is possible. Now, in the classics, "when properly taught," and in all genuine teaching, this dogmatic communication must be received, but received provisionally as a basis for further investigations, to be verified or disproved, as the pupil's experience and discerning powers increase. What, then, becomes of Mr. Spencer's argument for scientific education? Science, to be taught, must be "dogmatic" in its beginnings, or else becomes unteachable, and must "go."

Mr. Spencer lastly claims transcendent value for science against the classics as "information." But is physical science the only science? Is not man, is not humanity full of scientific phenomena? Is it not man's interest to know himself, in order to become what he ought to be, more than to know or do anything else? Are not his thoughts the expression of himself, and language the outside, of which all human thought is the inside? In this light, language is as worthy of scientific study as external nature.

7. Those who have suffered from erroneous methods of teaching. Here is the strongest source of attack. A great field is occupied by teachers mostly unacquainted with the art of teaching. In mathematics this difficulty is less troublesome. Everything there is "exactly right" or "exactly wrong." Method, the key to all education, lies on the surface and is simple rigorous deduction, constantly asserting itself and revenging its violations immediately. It is therefore easily acquired, and hence good elementary mathematical teachers are numerous and commercially cheap. Not so in classics. Here we encounter a grammar the most perfect yet discovered, constructed from languages rich to completeness in a vast variety of inflectional forms, with vocabularies where every word, even every word-element, indicates a distinct thought, with a syntax articulated to every imaginable kind and form of thinking; we meet a literature embracing acknowledged models in every style, and stored with the wisdom of a great civilization now passed away, but on which we stand. Method does not lie on the surface here. It must be hunted out with great pa-

tience, and needs thorough philosophical powers, first to discover, and next to apply it in teaching. Hence, good classical teachers are rare, and consequently expensive. Here the financial necessities of schools come in, and secure cheap teachers who, of course, do cheap teaching. Ignorant of the *rationale* of their subject, their pupils become still more so, and plod drearily along or else evade their tasks, receiving a minimum of benefit outweighed by a maximum of mental injury. Hence, many array themselves against the classics. Their hatred of the caricature is just; their enmity to the culture itself is deplorable.

II. The positive argument for classical training.

Every man's entire life is occupied with one continuous process of thought, of which the simplest, easiest, and one universal instrument is language. At the basis of knowledge lies the fact that we think of things. What we think is thought, and the expression of thought is language. If our thought tallies exactly with the thing thought of, we have an exactly correct thought, and if expression tallies with thought we have an exactly correct expression. Things underlie thought; thought underlies language. Here is the heart of the subject. Only as language and thought coincide, can knowledge itself be communicated and preserved; while so long as they are equivalent, language is as good as thought, just as a sound paper currency is as good as the gold it represents.

What does all this necessitate in education? Not teaching all languages. This is practically impossible. It therefore involves a selection of those best suited to accomplish the processes of education, — discipline and information. If, then, we can discover which languages these are, we must adopt them as the basis of all thorough literary education.

For educational purposes we make two classes, a man's native tongue and foreign languages. The first we must know, of course, as it is our chief means of intercourse. But we need more, both to understand English itself and enlarge our range of knowledge and so obtain completeness of power. Hence we need foreign languages. These are of two sorts, ancient and modern. From the first class all are prepared to rule out Oriental languages. What remains? Latin and Greek, the two fundamental languages of European culture wherever it has spread. From the second we rule out as unessential all except French and German. I firmly believe we can teach all four, — Latin, Greek, French, German, — with English as well, under any well-ordered system, and if we could not, modern languages might easily be acquired outside of our schools.

However, I ground the claim of the classical languages to a preëminent place on their immense superiority over all other languages, living or dead, as means of mental discipline. Let us hear Mr. Mill's argument for this:

"Even as mere languages, no modern European language is so valuable a discipline to the intellect as those of Greece and Rome, on account of their very regular and complicated structure. Consider for a moment what grammar is. It is the most elementary part of logic. It is the beginning of the analysis of the thinking process. The principles and rules of grammar are the means by which the forms of language are made to correspond with the universal forms of thought. The distinctions between the various parts of speech, between the cases of nouns, the modes and tenses of verbs, the functions of participles, are distinctions in thought, not merely in words. Single nouns and verbs express objects and events, many of which can be cognized by the senses; but the modes of putting nouns and verbs together, express the relations of objects and events, which can be cognized only by the intellect; and each different mode corresponds to a different relation. The structure of every sentence is a lesson in logic. The various rules of syntax oblige us to distinguish between the subject and predicate of a proposition, between the agent, the action, and the thing acted upon; to mark when an idea is intended to modify a quality, or merely to unite with some other idea; what assertions are categorical, what only conditional; whether the intention is to express similarity or contrast, to make a plurality of assertions conjunctively or disjunctively; what portions of a sentence, though grammatically complete within themselves, are mere members or subordinate parts of the assertion made by the entire sentence. Such things form the subject matter of universal grammar; and the languages which teach it best are those which have the most definite rules, and which provide distinct forms for the greatest number of distinctions in thought, so that if we fail to attend precisely and accurately to any of these we cannot avoid committing a solecism in language. In

54

these qualities the classical languages have an incomparable superiority over every modern language, and over all languages, dead or living, which have a literature worth being generally studied."

So, too, in their value as literature. Mr. Mill continues:

"But the superiority of the literature itself, for purposes of education, is still more marked and decisive. Even in the substantial value of the matter of which it is the vehicle, it is very far from having been superseded. The discoveries of the ancients in science have been greatly surpassed, and as much of them as is still valuable loses nothing by being incorporated in modern treatises; but what does not so well admit of being transferred bodily, and has been very imperfectly carried off, even in piecemeal, is the treasure which they accumulated of what may be called the wisdom of life; the rich store of experience of human nature and conduct, which the acute and observing minds of those ages, aided in their observations by the greater simplicity of manners and life, consigned to their writings, and most of which retains all its value. Their writings are replete with remarks and maxims of singular good sense and penetration, applicable both to political and to private life; and the actual truths we find in them are even surpassed in value by the encouragement and help they give us in the pursuit of truth.

"Human invention has never produced anything so valuable, in the way both of stimulation and of discipline, to the inquiring intellect, as the dialectics of the ancients, of which many of the works of Aristotle illustrate the theory and those of Plato exhibit the practice. No modern writings come near to these in teaching, both by precept and example, the way to investigate truth on those subjects, so vastly important to us, which remain matters of controversy from the difficulty or impossibility of bringing them to a directly experimental test. To question all things; never to turn away from any difficulty; to accept no doctrine, either from ourselves or from other people, without a rigid scrutiny by negative criticism, letting no fallacy or incoherence or confusion of thought slip by unperceived; above all, to insist upon having the meaning of a word clearly understood before using it, and the meaning of a proposition before assenting to it; these are the lessons we learn from the ancient dialecticians. With all this vigorous management of the negative element, they inspire no skepticism about the reality of truth or indifference to its pursuit. The noblest enthusiasm, both for the search after truth and for applying it to its highest uses, pervades these writers, Aristotle no less than Plato, though Plato has imcomparably the greater power of imparting those feelings to others. In cultivating, therefore, the ancient languages as our best literary

education, we are all the while laying an admirable foundation for
ethical and philosophical culture.

"In purely literary excellence, in perfection of form, the preëminence of the ancients is not disputed. In every department which
they attempted — and they attempted almost all — their composition,
like their sculpture, has been to the greatest modern artists an example to be looked up to with hopeless admiration, but of inappre-
ciable value as a light on high guiding their own endeavors."

Has not Mr. Mill covered the whole case?

III. The reasons for retaining Greek as well as Latin.

1. There is time to teach both without injuring other studies.
This has been abundantly proved in the Prussian gymnasia, or
classical schools. Latin and Greek form the central core of
instruction, occupying half their entire time. They also teach
the Christian religion, German, French, history, geography,
arithmetic, algebra, plane and solid geometry, plane trigonome-
try, natural history, physics, writing, drawing, music, gymnastics. Where do they save time for this? Mainly in mathematics
and physical science, which receive jointly less than half the
time given Latin and Greek, or but a trifle more than is given
Greek alone.

We should imitate the German example. First, by lessening
the excessive time devoted to such study, for example, as arithmetic. In some States it has received over half the entire
schooltime in certain years. Why should mathematics, either in
general or in particular, receive three times the attention it
receives in Germany? Second, we should teach Greek better,
both before and in college. Here time is saved by really using
it. Our trouble is not too much Greek, but too much badly
taught Greek.

2. Two important languages are better than one. Especially
is this true in Latin and Greek, whose differences are even
more remarkable than their resemblances.

3. While these differences give Latin a directer connection
with our civilization, yet Greek offers a finer instrument for
personal culture. Latin is the mother of modern tongues, the
language of law, history, empire, practical energy, collective

movements of men. But Greek is the mother-tongue of pure thought, the perfect instrument of human reason. The inexhaustible source for deriving the newest scientific terms to record the latest advances of thought in other languages, it yet never seeks to borrow for itself. It is subtler and more exact than Latin, more distinct in separate forms, more complex in masses, and more intimate in its mental attitude.

4. The Greek spirit, best studied at its original sources, is distinctively the great incentive to high creative effort in art. Antique sculpture and architecture — indispensable to art-students to-day — were its early children. Homer was its first poet, and his spell has worked in every world-renowned epic since. Its light was hidden in the Dark Ages, but when the Reformation unlocked man's conscience, the Florentine Greeks unlocked his intellect. Canova, Leonardo da Vinci, Raphael, Michael Angelo, — these were but Greeks late born. Greek rhythms rule modern music. Read the scores of Palestrina, any fugue of Bach, or Beethoven's symphonies. Read Wagner's great letter on "The Music of the Future." All are Greek throughout.

5. It is the truly scientific spirit. Not that the Greeks observed so many facts, but that they taught the world how to think. Huxley to-day vindicates Aristotle's scientific acuteness. Agassiz has shown that he also observed important facts about Mediterranean fishes, and, though the fishes remained abundant, the facts were only brought to light in modern times by consulting Aristotle's work. The facts were the same; the observers were not Aristotles. Passing these minutiae, look at our standard scientific conceptions: "ideas," "method," "theory," "practice," "hypothesis," "energy," "atoms," and the nomenclature of science, — all essentially Greek. Examine conflicting schools of thought. All have Greek prototypes. Men to-day are naturally what the Greeks first were historically, — stoics and epicureans, dogmatists and skeptics, materialists and idealists, agnostics and theists, and battle in the endless war of ideas bequeathed from their Greek ancestors. The stream of history is one. Who shall divide it?

6. Lastly, Latin itself is injured by separating it from Greek. Withdrawing Greek means crippling Latin. This helps to disintegrate classical culture, and so disastrously affects liberal education. As to the injury done Latin. This follows from the relations of the two languages, but I pass this and again appeal to the invaluable experience of Germany. The studies of the Gymnasia have been already stated. Alongside of this stands the Realschule, whose general make-up is the same, except that, though Latin is retained, Greek is dropped, English and chemistry added, and mathematics and science increased one-half. In revised plans of instruction issued in 1882 for secondary schools, by the Ministry of Education, and containing criticisms on the past twenty-five years' experience, these comments occur: "In the Realschulen the result from the Latin instruction by no means corresponds either with the amount of time devoted to it or to the importance assigned this instruction in the general plan of these institutions." This arises from the small number of hours given Latin, and from the excess of natural science which has proved "decidedly disadvantageous." No such complaints arise about gymnasial teaching either of Latin or science. Wherein does the Realschule fail? Just where it differs from the Gymnasia—that is, in the absence of Greek and consequent excess of science. "The main point," says the "Opinion" of the University of Berlin, "is that the instruction given in the Realschule lacks a central point; hence the unsteadiness in its system of teaching. . . . In a word, it has not been possible to find an equivalent for the (two) classical languages as a center of instruction."

As to the injury done to liberal education. The prove this I take the best test in the world,—comprehensive educational experience of undoubted authority. In 1870 the Prussian Ministry of Education determined to try the experiment of granting university privileges to Realschulen graduates alongside of those coming from Gymnasia. After over ten years of such trial, the Philosophical Faculty of the University of Berlin has recorded its judgment on the matter in an "Opinion" addressed to the Ministry of Education. This is the central faculty of the university, including all departments except Law, Medicine, and Theology. It numbers over one hundred instructors, and provides about two hundred courses of lectures. It enrolls such names as Helmholtz the physicist, Kirchhoff in spectrum analysis, Hofmann in chemistry, Ranke and Droysen in history, Mommsen and Curtius in the classics, and Zeller in philosophical criticism. If we desired a supreme court of culture to decide the classical question, to what better tribunal could we appeal than this? — the central faculty of the most illustrious university of the best educated nation in the world. Its judgment, always weighty, is here simply irresistible, because based upon careful investigation, and unanimous.

The "Opinion" rests upon the testimony of those instructors who have taught Realschule and Gymnasia graduates together. These are the professors of mathematics, astronomy, chemistry, descriptive natural science, philosophy, economics, statistics, and modern languages. Their testimony, detailed with great clearness, is strongly adverse to allowing Realschule graduates a continuance of university privileges. Many grave evils due to their admission are enumerated, and the Faculty expresses the conviction that, unless Prussia is ready to surrender her historic university system, "it is doubly hazardous" to shut their eyes to causes that, unchecked, will bring about this deplorable result. The essence of their judgment is in these words:

"The preparatory education acquired in Realschulen is, taken altogether, inferior to that guaranteed by the Gymnasia." This is for many reasons, "but above all, because the ideality of the scientific sense, interest in learning not dependent on nor limited by practical aims, but ministering to the liberal education of the mind as such, the many-sided and widely extended exercise of the thinking power, and an acquaintance with the classical bases of our civilization can be satisfactorily cultivated only in our institutions of classical learning." Such is the strongest plea yet made for classical education in all its integrity. Is it sufficient? If not, what can be?

Greek need not go. Let it remain. Rather let it begin to come.

It was born in the morning of history. Mythology fabled that its heroes were the children of immortals, and the records of humanity promise to confirm that claim. It schooled antiquity; it has been the historic safeguard for freedom of thought; it awakened the modern mind; it contains the most precious literary treasures of the race. Its corporeal form—the ancient civilization—has perished. Its material works of art, of priceless value, survive only in the crumbling column, the ruined temple, or the statue insecurely housed in some museum against Vandals of future time. But its best monument is its literature, multiplied a thousand-fold by the printer's art and imbedded in succeeding civilized thought. This still remains to challenge mankind in "charmed accents." In the pages of its texts, saved by centuries of diligence, the scholar by his quiet lamp reads back, through long perspectives of perfect thought, to the very beginnings of things intellectual. He gains a viewpoint where all lines of his intellectual being center and whence they broadly radiate. He sees the past sweeping on through the present and flowing widely into the far future. He sees that humanity, both individually and in the mass, is thus always one, and its generations, separate in time, united in nature; and so, instead of studying Greek because it is Greek, he studies it to understand himself.

3

What Is Academic Freedom?

Andrew F. West

The proposal recently urged by President Eliot that "in a university the student should choose his studies and govern himself," coupled with recent legislation at Harvard founded upon this principle, forces upon our American colleges a crisis greater than any they have hitherto been called upon to meet; greater not only for the reason that it affects the arrangement of their courses of study and their methods of government, but also because, if the real intention of the movement for which this skillfully worded proposal serves as a watchword and catchword is to prevail generally, our colleges must be reconstructed, their attitude as to conduct and studies radically changed, the objects for which they were founded set aside, the course of preparation for entrance greatly modified, and a system of training hitherto prevalent in education abandoned. The roots of this question extend to the very theory of education, to our fundamental beliefs both as to knowledge and morals, to the questions of intelligence and enlightenment in society. The proposal itself consists of two distinct parts—one that there is a stage in education when the student should be free to choose his studies and govern himself, the other that the university is the place where this freedom should be granted.

Reprinted from *North American Review*, Vol. 140, No. 342, May 1885, pp. 432-444.

These two statements no educated man will be apt to deny. The proposal (if this be all there is in it) is a harmless truism, a matter of general admission. But it has a purpose. It is no mere reassertion of a sound educational maxim; for the movement it represents expressly proposes to apply this to the American college, which is not in any sense a university, and has no early prospect of becoming one. Believing the proposal, though plausible in words, to be in the first place thoroughly unsound in theory, in the second place contrary to the best educational experience, and in the third place practically inapplicable to all or any of our existing colleges, I desire to examine it briefly by these three tests:

I. The proposal is unsound in theory. This takes us back, step by step, to the fundamental question from which all the others spring—Why do men need to be educated at all? The answer to this is very simple, almost too simple to repeat. It is part of the accepted alphabet of civilization. Men need to be educated because they are born into this world ignorant— ignorant of themselves and ignorant of the world in which they are to live. To live rationally and order their conduct wisely, they need to know; and being ignorant, they have to learn; and being ignorant and having to learn, they must be educated. But what do they need to know? Just that of which they are born ignorant, namely, themselves and their surroundings. If either of these two is left unexplored, the man is so far uninformed, ignorant, uneducated. A true education will therefore acquaint us with ourselves and with our surroundings. How is this to be done? In two ways. First, by training the mind to its highest efficiency, making it able both to know and to use all its powers to their full capacity. These as they unfold should therefore be exercised regularly, continuously, symmetrically. Thus, by frequent practice, the observing faculties are made acute and memory retentive, imagination is chastened, reason expanded, the will invigorated, the moral sense made clear, and the emotional nature kept unperverted and wholesome. In this way, and by the play of one power on the other, are built up such qualities as the logically clear judgment, the habit of industry, general command of our abilities, delicate taste, genuine tact, and, in short, all those ripened results in character which prove our capacity to act as free, well-balanced, rational men, able to decide for ourselves the thousand important questions of knowledge and conduct. Second, by communication of the most valuable knowledge. The training of the mind is not the sole object and process in education. The acquisition of useful, usable knowledge is also an end; for we have to live and make our way in the world. Hence this second part; it is a chief end for which we train our minds. But the training should come first, for it gives us the power to acquire. The supposed acquisitions, the observations and reasonings and the actions too, of a man of untrained mind are ignorant, crude, and intellectually worthless. When once the pupil has received this training, and thereby has attained sufficient maturity to know his powers accurately and use them wisely, he is ready for freedom, and not sooner. With this stage in his educational development properly comes the place where his freedom should be exercised, and that, by common consent, is the university. Is it for an instant to be supposed that our American boys, even from the best preparatory schools, are thus intellectually and morally mature when they enter college? Is it not a fact perfectly obvious to every one that knows anything about our colleges, that the reverse is true? Inexperience, immaturity, incomplete preparation, want of acquaintance with his own powers, half-shaped desires and purposes, with a conscious willingness on the part of the diligent to be trained and taught, —these are the very marks by which the entering freshman is regularly detected. Anything opposite to this is exceptional. Ask the alumni of any college what they were when they left school to become freshmen; ask preparatory instructors, college professors, who are concerned with teaching; parents, who know with what solid?tude they trusted their sons to the college; in fact, all who are in any way experts, and they give but one answer: The American college-student at entrance is decidedly immature.

It will be urged against this view that the way to mature him is to expect manly actions and intelligence, and thus elevate him by what we distinctly assume that he will do. Give the immature young student freedom at the very start, and this will bring out his sense of responsibility, and in this way will compel him to rise to self-possession, discriminating judgment, and intellectual ripeness. It is hard to say whether the chief characteristic of this view is its plausibility or its absurdity. Absurd it certainly is, for it attempts to bring out mental maturity, not by a training process but by a forcing process. It overlooks the prime law of mental development, which is that of continuous gradual growth, and not strained and sudden change. Shall we then seek to have students do what they have as yet no mature deliberative capacity for doing, by simply expecting it, or by further training? Clearly the latter. Can we omit or force any stages of mental growth, and leap from one plane to the other? Is not the mind to follow its own gradual and steady processes of development? The further objection, that in making a unversity we are entitled to count not only on what already exists, but on what may reasonably be expected of preparatory schools in response to the greater stimulus offered by increased requirements and expectations, has the same radical defect. In fact, the new departure at Harvard offers no such stimulus. The news that a boy may soon be able to enter there, and at graduation receive the degree of Bachelor of Arts, the symbol of academic culture, without ever having opened a Greek book, or, if he prefer, a Latin book, will not stimulate schools to require higher training. The additional fact that, save in freshman year, he may now go through and receive his degree without being required to take a single course in Latin, Greek, mathematics, physics, chemistry, geology, astronomy, psychology, logic, ethics, political science, German, or even English, is still less encouraging.* But suppose the movement to be a real attempt to secure higher preparation by having the unversity require this of the schools. Few if any

* See President McCosh's address on "The New Departure," p. 13. (New York, 1885).

of them are able to respond to severer requirements, such as the German, or even the French and English, schools consider necessary. Our best schools rarely furnish more than four years of Latin and three of Greek, taught at most five times a week. Compare with this the English six years' Latin and five Greek, or the French seven years' Latin and five years' Greek, both French and English schools giving these languages more exercises a week than we do. Are we ready to do this? Shall we ask it, and then simply expect it? For ten years Harvard has asked better English from our schools, and, as President Eliot confesses, with but indifferent success; and this is the verdict of colleges generally. But let us go a step higher in our comparison. Take the German gymnasia, with their nine years' Latin averaging nine exercises a week, and six years' Greek at the rate of six exercises a week. Besides this, there are eight years of French and nine years of training in the mother-tongue. Is it not folly to talk of obtaining anything comparable to this by merely requiring and expecting it of our existing schools? Schools do not stand on colleges, but colleges on schools. The higher limit of preparatory teaching will fix the lower limit for colleges or universities. As this moves up or down, they move with it. To use the words of Prof. Hofmann, of Berlin: "The form and contents of university instruction will always be dependent on the amount of preparation that the student brings with him to the university." * Education grows from below upward, from the elementary to the advanced, and each lower stage needs substantial completion before the next higher can be essayed with reasonable hope of success. What the student "brings with him" from the lower, gives him confidence in attempting the higher.

II. The proposal is opposed to the best educated experience of the world. Systems of education have been built. Generations of well-tested experience are at hand for our inspection. This is no new question. The universities of the Old World have had to meet it. Three great systems have been construct-

* Inaugural address as Rector of the University, Oct. 15, 1880.

ed, — the English, the French, and the German, — and each of them on a well-defined basis. The English universities stand on the endowed public schools with their six years' course, whose central core is classical and mathematical preparation, with thorough training in the moral qualities of diligence and obedience to law. The French university plan is a system of special faculties, and the University of Paris a commission of expert educators, who prescribe the preparatory course for the lycées. These have a seven years' course, classical and mathematical at heart, and upon this stands the higher education of France. The German, or, more correctly, the Prussian university system is confessedly the best of all that have hitherto appeared. It stands on the gymnasium. President Eliot wishes us to take humble lessons from Germany as to what universities ought to be; and to that court the case may well be submitted as to that of the best qualified judges in the world. What is the Prussian system? What are its guarantees of university stability and efficiency? They are three.

First. At the base of the whole fabric lies compulsory education, given in the Volkschule.

Second. Next above this stands the gymnasium. This has a nine years' continuous course of study. Its instruction centers in the classical languages, Latin being taught nine years, with an average of nine weekly exercises, and Greek six years, with six lessons a week. These two form nearly half of all the school work. To this we must add nine years of the mother-tongue, taught fully three times a week, and eight of French twice a week. This completes the language-instruction, which in all amounts to about eighteen lessons a week. Twenty lessons is the approximate weekly work of our American schools. But this is only two-thirds of the German schedule. Add two exercises more for religious instruction, five for mathematics and elementary science, three for history and geography, two for writing and drawing, and we have the gymnasial schedule of thirty lessons a week,* an amount not paralleled elsewhere.

* *Centralblatt fur die gesammte Unterrichts Verwaltung in Breussen,* April, 1882.

Besides this, there are gymnastics and music. At the end of the course, if the pupil desires to enter the university regularly and seek a degree at graduation, he must first pass the severe *Abiturienten-examen,* or final examination of the school. The object of this is distinctly prescribed, namely, "to ascertain whether the student has attained to that degree of scholarly culture which is the goal of the gymnasium." * To this end all cramming is severely discouraged, all roundabout ways, short cuts, or extraordinary efforts before examination, are excluded so far as possible, and reliance is placed on the quietly sustained work of the long school course. The examination is conducted by a carefully organized commission, and has two parts, the written and the oral, of which the written lasts a week. At the end of the examination the successful student's reward is the *Zeugniss der Reife,* the "certificate of ripeness" or maturity, which alone can insure him a place in the university as a regularly matriculated student, a candidate for the degree at the end of his university career. This certificate is most carefully drawn. It always contains three things — a statement as to the student's moral behavior, attentiveness, and diligence, a statement as to how his recitation and examination attainments have comported with the standard of the school, and a declaration that he has sustained the final examination. Armed with this proof of "ripeness," he is ready, in the judgment of the Prussian university, for university freedom, but not sooner.

The gymnasium does even more than this. Not content with training and testing its pupils, it also proves its teachers. Ordinarily the Prussian gymnasial teacher must first have passed through the gymnasium as a pupil, and after that the university, where, if he wishes to stand well, he attends the *Seminar* or regular meeting for training and investigation in his department, and takes a degree at the end of his course upon a stringent examination, and at all events passes the terrible *Staatsexamen,* on which depends his right to be employed as a teacher. If he runs all these gauntlets, he passes a trial-year or

* Id., May, 1882, p. 377.

Probe-jahr at teaching. Then, if successful, he is entitled to call himself a teacher. These are the men that make the gymnasium what it is, "the corner-stone of German culture."*

Third. As the gymnasium rests upon the Volkschule, so the university in turn rests upon the gymnasium and crowns the whole system. Here the student is free. As Helmholtz, in his address† as Rector at Berlin, explains it, the students are "young men responsible to themselves, striving after science of their own free will, to whom it is left to arrange their own plan of studies as they think best." Here is freedom in studies and conduct, and at the university. But this freedom does not mean that any student, even if he be a gymnasial graduate, will obtain his degree at the end of his course, no matter what subjects he studies. If he desires a degree, he must first obtain permission to be examined, and then present himself thoroughly prepared in some one chief subject, called his *Hauptfach,* in which he must show, not mere accomplishments, but that he has done original investigation. Besides this, he must offer one or two kindred subsidiary subjects, called *Nebenfächer.* Should he venture to present absurdly unrelated subjects, such as chemistry and Sanskrit, the university would refuse to examine him. Should he seek for such subjects as French plays and novels, courses giving facility in Spanish or Italian, or the beginnings of fine art, he would search in vain to find them in a Prussian university.‡ And whether he seeks a degree or not, if he wishes to fill any of the offices of church or state, he must still pass the *Staats-examen,* whose power is well-nigh absolute, and whose rigor is unrelenting. This upholds the whole level of university work, in addition to the guarantees furnished from below by the gymnasium. Such is the Prussian university, and such its pledges of stability. First the Volkschule, then the gymnasium, after that the university. Need we wonder that the

* Opinion of the University of Berlin, (Boston, 1883.)
† "On Academic Freedom in German Universities," delivered October 15, 1877.
‡ For complete lists of all the courses offered in the German universities, consult the *Deutscher Universitat Kalender,* published in Berlin.

Germans are profoundly attached to it and regard it as the very crown of their civilization?

It is almost superfluous to say that President Eliot's proposed university has not one of these three great safeguards. All the features considered essential by the Germans are lacking. Still more, the practical interpretation of the proposal — seen in the intention to make Greek or Latin optional for entrance, whereas the Germans consider these two the essentials, or rather the one indivisible essential, of preparatory training — is calculated to lower our already insufficient standards. Of the same character is the attempt first to dissipate and consequently degrade the meaning of the degree of Bachelor of Arts, the historic symbol of college culture, by using it to label graduation in hundreds of combinations of different studies, from the severest to the easiest, and then to call it a university degree; whereas the Germans have no Bachelor of Arts degree, but intend by their degrees, such as Ph. D., to label ability for original investigation only, and not miscellaneous attainments. This is not improvement and advancement of our already imperfect education, but the disintegration of even what good we now have. The lesson of Germany and of England and of France for us is, not to build universities high in the clouds and try to drag up the foundations toward them, but to find the foundation first and then build in full faith that the structure will stand.

It is a singular fact that the French Revolution, that great leveler of good and bad alike, destroyed the old classical training of France. The experiment of destruction was seen to be a mistake, and if the last and present generation of French educators have devoted themselves to anything with success, it has been to the reëstablishment of the lyceés. It is also to be remembered that in the early years of this century Prussia tried the plan of admitting to university privileges students whose maturity was not guaranteed by the gymnasia. The distress that followed the Napoleonic wars forced universities to let down their bars, and they did so with disastrous effects, notably at the University of Bonn. This produced a strong reaction, and out of this very crisis emerged the present system in full play a few years later, under the leadership of Von Humboldt, Minister of Education, who cut out the pernicious practice by the roots and lodged the great power of the *Abiturienten-examen* in the gymnasia,* thus holding gymnasial training unbroken to its completion. From that time dates the manhood of the Prussian university. The spirit of President Eliot's movement was tested and condemned in Prussia long before it was born here.

More widely known than either of these is the experiment recently allowed by the Prussian universities under protest, that of admitting students without gymnasial preparation as candidates for degrees. It is well to remember that the Realschule pupils, thus allowed to enter, whose preparation the universities consider fatally deficient, simply differ from gymnasial graduates in having no Greek, less Latin (though they have nine years of it), and more modern languages, mathematics, and science. The opinion of the University of Berlin on this question is so well known as to need no special comment; it is unmistakable and unanimous. A few words from Hofmann and Helmholtz, professors there, both of the first scientific eminence, and both recently honored with the dignity of Rector of that university, will be of weight here. This is from Hofmann, on the character and secret of gymnasial success:

"After a long and vain search; we must always come back finally to the result of centuries of experience, that the surest instrument that can be used in training the mind of youth is given us in the study of the languages, the literature, and the works of art of classical antiquity."

And this is from Helmholtz, on academic freedom:

"Any institution based upon freedom must also be able to calculate upon the judgment and reasonableness of those to whom freedom is granted . . . . The majority of students must come to us with a sufficiently logically trained judgment, with a sufficient habit of mental exertion, with a tact sufficiently developed on the best models, to be able to discriminate truth from the babbling appear-

---

* See Matthew Arnold's "Higher Schools and Universities of Germany," ed. of 1874, chapter on the *Abiturienten-examen.*

ance of truth. . . . Thus prepared, they have hitherto been sent to us by the gymnasiums. It would be very dangerous for the universities if large numbers of students frequented them who were less developed in these respects. The general self-respect of the students must not be allowed to sink. If that were the case, the dangers of academic freedom would choke its blessings. It must not, therefore, be looked upon as pedantry, or arrogance, if the universities are scrupulous in the admission of students of a different style of education."*

III. The proposal is practically inapplicable to our existing colleges, any or all of them. The essential feature of the American college is a four years' course of study leading to the degree of Bachelor of Arts. A college may have many other courses besides this, — scientific, literary, or special, — but this one is its historic center, and has been its strength. Acquaintance with our current college catalogues and college history cannot fail to prove the truth of this fact. On what does the college stand? On preparatory schools that rarely, if ever, given more than four years to their special preparation, four years for Latin, and the last three of these four to Greek also. Until within a few years, the college course of study has been prescribed throughout. But as our schools have improved, the leading colleges have been able to allow limited freedom of choice for part of the studies of the last two college years, and have kept the first two entirely or substantially prescribed, with their classical and mathematical training and incidental teaching in modern languages and science, — the very elements of gymnasial instruction. If we take four years of preparatory training with the first two years of prescribed training in college, we find six years of fairly disciplinary education, running to the end of sophomore year. From this time such colleges as Yale and Princeton introduce the elective system, but preserve with it a substratum of prescribed studies. This is the attitude of our colleges generally. Harvard, however, has now no required courses except three in freshman year, —

* "On Academic Freedom in German Universities," Inaugural" Address as Rector at Berlin, Oct. 15, 1877.

one in English, one in modern languages, and one in elementary science,—and these bid fair to vanish soon, and thus leave a complete system of election, subject only to restrictions of college convenience in teaching and the unwillingness that individual instructors may exhibit to open their particular courses to unprepared students.

This system goes still further. All uniformity of studies being removed, the students choose as they wish among the hundreds of possible combinations; and whatever be the character of their courses chosen, severe or easy, rationally connected or wildly miscellaneous, they are all entitled upon examination to receive the degree of Bachelor of Arts. This, instead of meaning one definite thing, may now indicate hundreds of different kinds of courses. Besides thus affecting the degree with which the college stamps its approval on its graduates at the end, it also affects the entrance itself. For if the student may drop all his disciplinary school studies upon entering freshman year, the preparatory four years of Latin and three of Greek (or, as is more commonly the case, three of Latin and two of Greek), if stopped here, are fragmentary and incomplete, worth little to those who pursue them no further. Hence Greek, having received the least time, was attacked first and made optional. Now Latin also is made optional. The student, as he prefers, is to offer one, but need not bring both, in order to enter and gain the degree at the end. The irresistible logic of the situation will not permit this to stop here. When Greek goes, why does it go? Because it has had but slight attention at the school, and as it need not be pursued in college and is not a prerequisite for the degree, and hence at best only a fragment, it goes. But the system allows Latin to be omitted, on condition that the student offers Greek. Latin, it is true, usually receives a year more than Greek in the schools; but as the student need not continue Latin, it is also a fragment. If the student may drop both Latin and Greek as he enters college, why compel him to offer both, or one, or either, in order to enter? Either alone is a fragment of no great value, both together are incomplete unless pursued further. There is no good reason, and so the next thing to go after Greek or Latin will be Greek and Latin; and who shall insure the movement stopping even here?

What, then, is the situation? Simply this: the proposal that comes disguised as an alluring plea for universities, and consequent university freedom, first destroys the meaning of our only existing degree given for academic culture, by making it mean everything, and so nothing. It abolishes not only the prescribed substratum of studies commonly found in the last two years of college, but also the prescribed training of the first two years. Thereupon, instead of making every effort to secure what is thus lost from the college (or attempted university) by strengthening the schools so that they may make good the deficiency, it not only makes no such attempt, but, by making Latin or Greek optional for the boy who is to enter, it puts a premium on the avoidance of these studies which the best experience of the world assures us are the very essentials of high preparation, and so degrades our already imperfect school training. In short it means not the construction of a real university, but the destruction of what little good we now have in our preparatory education. It means the creation of a so-called university to which students shall be attracted by the plea of freedom, but a place where no strong guarantee of training preliminary to entrance is required, and no assurance of scholarship expect for its degree; a place where young students may flock from our schools without a common basis of culture, and may study what they please, as they please, if they please; a place where thousands may come to sit under the shadow of a university and get what they desire, with none to molest or make them afraid—only to discover, too late, that no university has ever cast its shadow upon them. Is this the promotion of higher culture? Is this liberal education? Is this what educated experience counsels? Is there any assurance that such a fabric will contain one element of intellectual unity, strength, or permanence?

It is the part of wisdom to take another plan. Strengthen and improve the good we now have, crude and defective though it be. Build from the base upward, and not from the clouds downward. Make better schools, train better teachers, study a few things well and continuously, and lift the whole level of our preparatory education. Then will the university, so deeply needed at this time in our American life, not only be a possibility but a certainty.

Freedom in studies, freedom in conduct. I have spoken mainly of the first, but these two are one. It is one education of one mind acting and interacting in two lines. The attainments in culture are moral attainments, and conversely. The very means employed to produce intellectual education and the desired products of this education are moral. Discipline in studies is out of the question, unless the moral elements of diligence, attentiveness, candor, ready obedience to law, determination to achieve honorable success, patience, perserverance, courage, assured control over appetites and passions, and unselfish devotion to pending duty are the ruling powers. These are both preconditions and products of genuine education. He who has them not is in the worst sense uneducated. What might such a man as Byron have been if, as Goethe (no prejudiced witness here) asserts, "he had but known how to endure moral restraint also? That he could not, was his ruin." What may, what do men become when thus destitute? Does not the proposal for freedom in conduct touch this question deeply? It is urged that the college is not to teach religion or attempt the supervision of morals. Let the student look to these himself, aided by the natural helps of home remembrances, his studies, and his ambition. If this be so, and the home-training in religion and virtue, priceless so far as it goes, is to cease when the inexperienced American school-boy becomes a freshman, and finds that religion which he has been taught to revere receiving no public recognition or general respect from the college, and instruction in religion specifically ruled out from the course of study, that the college in no way encourages him to attend any religious exercise, that in matters of morals he cannot confidently expect the personal help and succor of his instructors in his various endeavors to

74

act honorably, live purely, and resist temptations to evil that will meet him just as surely as his college days go on, — if this easy-going dealing with faith and morals is the spirit of the new departure, it is certainly the most dangerous element in the whole movement. That this is its spirit, is clear from its record. We must judge it not by what it hopes or expects or promises, but by what it has done, and these things are matters of observation.

Our hopes lie another way. What our youth most need is discipline of character, deeply inwrought with their studies. What our culture needs is men first and specialists second; otherwise, we shall not avoid the intellectual horrors that lie in exclusive specialism in one direction and dilettanteism in the other. What our society needs is a large number of trained, enlightened men, the only sure guarantee for an enlightened public opinion. If these things are true, then let those who believe them resist and expose this new departure, not in, but from education.

4

American Colleges
and German Universities

Richard T. Ely

Many excellent articles and addresses on college and university education in the United States and Germany have been written during the last ten years, but the authors have usually taken it for granted not only that all have clear ideas as to the character and purposes of these institutions, but also that perfect harmony exists between these ideas. The discussion has, therefore, turned upon the means of realizing a character and accomplishing ends not plainly defined. Had, however, each educational reformer first obtained a clear conception of the actual "final cause" of American and foreign universities and colleges, and then compared that conception with the desired "final cause," it is safe to assert that the present notions in respect to both would be far less confused.

The comparison universally made is between our colleges and the German universities. It is shown that the condition of higher education in the United States is in a sad state—and about this there can be no doubt; that in Germany, on the contrary, it is in a flourishing one; *ergo*, let us turn our colleges into German universities. The next question is, How? In answer to this it is explained that in the German universities the studies are all elective and optional; in the colleges of the

Reprinted from *Harper's New Monthly Magazine*, Vol. 61, No. 362, July 1880, pp. 253-260.

United States, compulsory. The conclusion is not difficult to be drawn. Make all studies in the colleges elective, and the work is done! The country is provided with a set of first-class universities! The German universities have thus been taken as models, and a sort of blind attempt made to imitate them in the way described. German universities are an acknowledged success, it is true; but what does it mean to pronounce an institution a success? It signifies that a harmony exists between the intentions of its founders and managers and the accomplished results. The questions then naturally arise, What is the purpose of the German university? What is its real distinguishing feature? Then, after having answered these, the further questions, Do American colleges have the same aims? If they do not, is it desirable that they should?

The answer to the first questions is not difficult. A German university is, from beginning to end, through and through, a professional school. It is a place where young men prepare to earn their "bread and butter," as the Germans say, in practical life. It is *not* a school which pretends or strives to develop in a general way the intellectual powers, and give its students universal culture. This is the first point which should be clearly understood by all trying to Germanize our institutions. As soon as the student enters the university he makes a selection of some one study or set of studies—law, medicine, theology, or some of the studies included in the "philosophical faculty" —chemistry, physics, Latin, Greek, philosophy, literature, modern languages, etc. If a student pursues chemistry, it is because his chemistry is to support him in after-life; if Latin and Greek, because he is preparing himself for a position as teacher; so it is with the other branches. The first question a university student asks before selecting a study is, "Of what practical benefit will this be to me?" An opportunity is given to extraordinary talent and genius of developing, however, by allowing a certain freedom in "learning and teaching." There is no regulation to prevent a student of law from hearing a lecture, *e. g.*, on the Agamemnon of Aeschylus; but this rarely happens. Each one has the examination in mind which is to

78

admit him into active life, and, as a rule, pursues only the studies required for passing it, and what is more, pursues them no farther than is likely to be demanded. If a smattering of the history of philosophy is required, as in the theological examination in Prussia, the candidate will read the little work by Schwegler, but stop there. There are exceptions: some study for the love of study, for the love of science, of truth; but they are few. The professors who teach sciences not required for some examination complain that comparatively few students attend their lectures. Professor Wundt, the distinguished psychologist and philosopher of Leipzig, explains in this way the little attention paid to philosophy by German students. In the philosophical magazine *Mind,* for November, 1877, he compares the German and English universities. "The German student does not," says he, "like his English compeer, reside at the university simply with the object of general scientific culture, but, first and foremost, he pursues a 'Brodstudium.' He has chosen a profession which is to procure him a future living as doctor, practicing lawyer, clergyman, master in one of the higher schools, or the like, and for which he must establish his fitness in an examination at the close of his university career. But how enormously have the subjects of instruction increased in the majority of these professions!...... It requires either compulsion or a specially lively interest to bring our doctors, lawyers, philologists, to the philosophical lectures. But of late compulsion has for the most part ceased." Professor Wagner, the political economist, of Berlin, has not long since expressed himself quite similarly. He says only a small number of the law students hear his lectures on political economy, or any other lectures which are not absolutely required for examination. In the University of Berlin there are over three thousand matriculated students, and nearly two thousand nonmatriculated attendants at lectures; but so celebrated a man as Zeller has only a small number of hearers at his lectures on psychology, because it is a subject required for but few examinations. At Halle in the winter semester 1877-78 only one course of lectures on psychology was announced, that, however, by a clever young man, an author of some philosophical works. Although there are nine hundred students at Halle, the lectures were not delivered, because two could not be found who desired to hear them. The only one who presented himself was the writer, a foreigner, and when he was trying to find number two, and proposed to others to hear the lecture, the answer was, "It is not required for the examination."

This shows how seriously those college professors and trustees have erred who have imagined that they were turning our American colleges into German universities by making the studies elective and optional. The German institution which corresponds to an American college as a school of general intellectual training is the gymnasium, where there is but a minimum of election in the studies; e. g., Hebrew is optional, and the student has perhaps a choice between English and some other study. The Germans suppose that experienced teachers and men of tried ability, who have devoted years to investigating the matter, are better able to judge of the studies advisable for the general development of the intellectual powers of boys than the boys themselves. It would seem that they might be in the right. On the contrary, the essence of the freedom which each university student has of electing his studies is simply the freedom given to men of selecting their own professions. The door through which every German must pass into office or profession is the examination; but the Minister of Instruction and other public authorities prescribe very minutely the studies required for each examination. Each German student is required to have pursued certain sciences, differing according to his intended profession, before he can enter active life. He has only the liberty of pursuing them when, where, and in the order which he will. He selects his own books, professors, and has his own method. He may be five years in preparing for the examinations, or ten, if he chooses to waste time. This is truly a considerable liberty, but far less than it is generally supposed the German students enjoy. Professor Helmholtz, in his inaugural address, delivered

October 15, 1877, as rector of the University of Berlin, acknowledges that many German fathers and statesmen have demanded a diminution of even the existing liberty of university life, and adds, farther, that a stricter discipline and control of the students by the professors would undoubtedly save many a young man who goes to ruin under the present system.

There are three departments of our colleges or universities which correspond to three of those of the German universities, and offer no insurmountable difficulty in the perfection of our school system. These departments are those of law, theology, and medicine. The reforms necessary must be evident to men of the respective professions: greater freedom of the schools from the principle of private money-making institutions; a longer and more thorough course of study, as in Germany, where the time required to be passed in previous study for admittance to these professional schools. That here is a place where the government, if not the central, at least that of the separate States, has a duty to perform, no political economist where the government, if not the central, at least that of the separate States, has a duty to perform, no political economist or statesmen of note is so given to the *laissez-faire* principle as to deny. All of our States recognize this, and exercise some control as regards physicians and lawyers. If a tailor makes me a poor suit of clothes, no great harm is done: I try another next time. Besides, I can demand samples of his work beforehand, and even if no tailor myself, am not utterly unable to judge of his work. Here the principle of private competition is the only proper one. But the principle of private competition in respect of law and medicine is not sufficient. If a medical quack kills my child, it does not help the matter to reply to my complaints, "Well, try another doctor next time." It is heartless. My child is dead, and nothing can help the matter now. "But you should have known that the man was a humbug," says some one. I should have known nothing of the kind. It is precisely because I do not know, because I am no physician, that I require one. Again, in many small towns there is only one physician, and the people have no choice. It is the same case with lawyers.

An ignorant or incapable man may cause me the loss of my property, or even my neck. This "next time" theory helps the matter not at all. It is too late. There is for me no next time. The man appeared to me clever; he talked well, and I tried him. I judged as well as I could, but my not being a lawyer made it impossible for me to be a competent judge of his abilities. The State, then, does its citizens a real service, and one they can not do for themselves, in forcing candidates for the legal and medical professions to submit themselves to an examination by competent authorities, who pronounce upon their fitness for exercising the functions of lawyers or doctors. This principle is recognized by every civilized government in the world, though perhaps nowhere so laxly and negligently as in the United States. What is necessary, then, as regards these professional schools is for the State by proper legislation to raise the standard of requirements, and so assist the colleges and universities in giving us an able and properly educated set of professional men, as in Germany, where actual legal and medical malpractice are exceedingly rare. England has lately been forced to take a step in the right direction by making the requirements for becoming a physician severer. The profession was too open to the principle of free competition, and the abuses became intolerable. One other means of improving these professional schools would be to bring them in closer connection with the college departments, so that a medical or law student should have the liberty of hearing lectures on history, political economy, etc., if he wished. All the different schools should, of course, have one common library. This is the plan pursued on the continent of Europe. It frequently happens, too, that students of different departments have the same studies, and it is a waste of time, money, and force to separate them here. The law student is not the only one who needs to understand "international law," nor the medical student the only one who ought to have some knowledge of physiology and hygiene.*

* The writer does not consider theological schools, because that is a matter which each Church must take care of for itself, so long as

The so-called college department, or "college proper," is the one which offers most difficulty to the reformer, and the one where the most confusion prevails. When the course of study is simply one for general culture, it is no part of a university, in the continental European sense of that term. There is, therefore, in America a want of a school offering opportunities to large and constantly increasing classes of men for pursuing professional studies—a want which is deeply felt, and which sends every year many students and millions of dollars out of the country. Where in the United States can a young man prepare himself thoroughly to become a teacher of the ancient classics? A simple college course is not enough. The Germans require that their teachers of Latin and Greek should pursue the classics as a specialty for three years at a university after having completed the gymnasium, which as a classical school would be universally admitted to rank with our colleges. Every college professor of Latin and Greek must admit the need of better preparatory teachers. The poor entrance examinations, when the candidates for admissions do not come from some one of our few old and excellent but expensive academies, like Exeter, Andover, and the Boston Latin School, bear only too strong witness of their previous training. If an American wishes to pursue a special course in history, politics, political economy, mathematics, physics, philosophy, or in any one of many other studies lying outside of the three professions, law, medicine, and theology, he must go to Europe. Even to pursue the study of United States history, the American will do better to go abroad. From Maine to California, from Minnesota to Texas, there is no institution which teaches United States history thoroughly. Many colleges require no knowledge of it, either for entering or graduating. Others imagine that they have done their full duty in demanding a few historical names and dates as condition of admittance. As many—in the country the majority—of our

state and church are entirely separate. Where there are so many sects as in the United States it may be well that the schools of divinity should be by themselves.

lower schools do not teach history, the result is sad enough. English papers have with reason spoken slightingly of historical instruction in our country. Again, whoever desires, even in theology, medicine, or law, to select some one branch as a specialty, must go to Europe to do so. But these professional schools are already organized, and their needs recognized.

What is to be done about the college department? How get system out of the confusion of our system, or rather no system? for we have in the United States, with the exception of a few States, no school system, although some good schools.* Until we have adopted a satisfactory system, we may rest assured that thousands of parents will continue to educate their children in Europe.

We have the materials in the United States for a good school system, beginning in the common school and ending in the university; the need is organization. Dr. Barnard would have three grades—the school, academy, and college.† But should not a fourth be added—the university? It is not necessary that the university should be separate from the college, though in some places it might be, as in the Johns Hopkins University, which started with the intent of becoming a university. Harvard will serve as an illustration. If Harvard required a college education for entering any one of its departments, placing them all on a level, made all studies elective except in examination, and enlarged its curriculum so as to enable one to pursue spe-

* He who would be convinced of the unreason of our educational organization, can do no better than read the able and interesting address delivered by Andrew D. White, LL.D., now United States Minister at Berlin, before the National Educational Association at Detroit, August 5, 1874. It is entitled, "The Relations of the National and State Governments to Advanced Education," and published in pamphlet form by "Old and New," Boston.

† Dr. Barnard's position is not here accurately stated. In his Albany address he was considering general, and not professional, education; and his complaint was that the ground is taken away from under any possible university proper, in this country, by clothing every petty college with university powers.—Editor *Harper's Magazine*.

cial courses in Latin, Greek, political science, etc., it would become in every respect a professional school, *i. e.,* a university.* Those who entered would already have finished their general studies, and would go there to prepare for some particucular profession, as that of teacher of Latin and Greek, or some one or two of the natural sciences, or to become physician, editor, etc. Now it is different. Harvard *demands* very limited requirements for entering its professional schools, but *desires* that the students of these schools should first complete the college course of four years. So long as this is expected, it seems impossible that the requirements for admission to the college department should be raised. If a young man is eighteen years of age upon entering, he is not able to begin his professional studies before twenty-two, which makes him at least twenty-five upon entering practical life—quite old enough. Harvard's requirements for admission give the American student a rather longer course before beginning his professional career than is required from his German compeer, who commences them at twenty or thereabouts. If Harvard continues to increase its conditions for admission to the college department, it can not expect the lawyers, doctors, and clergymen to pursue just the college course. The result would be that more young men than at present would begin their professional studies without having previously pursued even an ordinary college course. The solution of the difficulty lies in rather diminishing than otherwise the requirements for admission to the college proper, or academic department, of Harvard, in

* The term university is here used in the sense in which it is, or has come to be, used in Germany. It is not the primary signification. The German universities have developed into professional schools, while the British, originally identical in form with those of the continent, have not undergone that development. Is not the power of conferring degrees, as Dr. Barnard suggests, the distinctive function of a university, *i.e.,* of a university in the European sense of the term? Are not all the elements that go to make a school a university simply those which fit it for the exercise of this function?—Editor *Harper's Magazine.*

putting the extra studies in the graduate courses, which latter form part of the university proper, and in requiring a college education at Harvard or some other good college as a condition of entering any department of the university. The writer would thus separate distinctly college education and university education. Their methods and aims are different. The college should adhere to its old plan, give thorough instruction in Latin, Greek, French, German, mathematics, general history, etc. The courses should be, for the most part, prescribed, and contain such studies as would fit young men for taking a position in society as educated gentlemen; then should follow business or professional studies. It would seem that this course ought to be finished at twenty, as Dr. McCosh recommends. In other countries the corresponding courses of study do not require more time, though in most the professional courses are longer and severer, as they will surely become in the United States, as they must become, in a time when all professions are making such strides, and the number of studies increased proportionately. If colleges, then, consecrated themselves to this more modest but more useful plan of becoming higher academies, and nothing more, we should find that our four hundred and twenty-five colleges were not such a great superfluity as we now think. Great laboratories, costly observatories, and apparatus indispensable to a university, would be entirely unnecessary. Thoroughness, of which there is now great lack, should be one of the main points. In some places in the West there would be still too many colleges, but by uniting in some places, and by a better local distribution in others, this could be remedied. Let us compare the statistics of two other countries, in which the excellence of higher instruction is admitted alike by friend and foe—France and Germany. In 1874 Germany had 333 gymnasia, besides 170 progymnasia and Latin schools. The progymnasia are a low grade of academy, but some of the Latin schools rank with the gymnasia. Since 1874 over twenty new gymnasia and progymnasia have been established. We can calculate, therefore, that Germany has at least 350 gymnasia or classical colleges. But besides these there were, in the beginning of the year 1874, 106 "Realschulen erster Ordnung," which have a curriculum similar to the Latin and scientific course of some of our colleges, as Cornell. Germany has, therefore, over 450 "colleges proper," scientific and classical, and is increasing the number. Germany's population is a trifle greater than that of the United States. Prussia, with less than 26,000,000 inhabitants, had, in 1874, seventy-nine "Realschulen erster Ordnung," with 23,748 scholars; 228 gymnasia, with 57,605 students; together, 81,353. It is not to be forgotten that the scholars enter the gymnasia and Realschulen when very young, so that the time required to complete the course is eight years. The programmes of these schools and the statistics seem to ars the rank of American college students, say, 25,000 in Prussia.

France, with a smaller population then the United States, has eighty lyceés, with 36,756 scholars, and 244 colleges, with 32,744 scholars; together, 69,500. These schools resemble German gymnasia, and we shall not probably be far out of the way in giving 20,000 of them the rank of American college students.

According to Dr. Barnard's statistics, as given in *Harper's Weekly,* the number of under-graduates in all American colleges is 18,000. We see that a greater proportion of the youth of France and Germany devote themselves to liberal studies than of America. Besides, there are over 19,000 university students in Germany, not to speak of those in the mining and technical schools, undoubtedly many more than in the graduate and professional schools in the United States. In France, in 1868, the attendance at university lectures amounted to 11,903. But in France the faculties have the right of holding examinations and granting diplomas. Twenty-seven thousand six hundred and thirty-four examinations were held in the same year; 9344 received diplomas.

As America becomes older and wealth increases, we might

expect, *a priori,* the proportionate number of Americans avail-
ing themselves of the advantages of higher education to increase. This is unfortunately not the case, as the careful statistics of Dr. Barnard too clearly demonstrate. Many reasons
can be given for this decrease. One may be the higher standard
required for admission by some of the best colleges. One
would hardly like to say that, abstractly considered, even Harvard's requirements were too severe, but they stand out of all
relation to the condition of the lower schools in the greater
part of the country. It is not daring to assert that there are
entire States in the Union where scarcely a suitable preparatory school for institutions like Harvard, Yale, and Columbia
exists. Now parents may be willing to send their sons away
from home at sixteen, but most fathers and mothers do not
like to do so when they are only ten years old. The remedy
lies in a better provision and more careful supervision of
grammar and high schools. It were very desirable that none but
college graduates, or those who should pass an examination
implying the same amount of knowledge as a college graduate
is expected to have, should be permitted to occupy the higher
positions in these schools. The government has manifestly
the same right to demand this that it has to require the present
minimum of knowledge. It seems childish to argue the question, but so many good people among us are blindly attached
to the *laissez-faire* principle of the last century that it may be
well to put one or two questions to them. What right has the
state to force those who wish to teach to pass any examination
at all? How can one limit this right, once conceded, so as to
make it meaningless? If the government has the duty of seeing that the rising generation is educated, why should it not
have the right of using such means as will enable it to accomplish its duty effectually? Nay, what right has the government
to use the people's money, or allow it to be used, in employ-
ing public servants who are incapable of performing their
duties efficiently? At present the requirements are so low that
the supply of teachers greatly exceeds the demand, and that
American has had an experience as happy as rare who has
not repeatedly seen brazen effrontery take the place away from

modest merit. The Germans, whom we often accuse of a lack of practical understanding, exhibit more common-sense in these matters than we. In Germany the requirements are proportioned to the grade of the teacher, and are kept so high that the demand for teachers is slightly in excess of the supply. There is thus a tendency toward a continual advance in quality. Every encouragement is offered to excellence, as it is rewarded proportionately. Another probable cause of the small number of college students is the discredit brought on higher education by Western institutions like the "universities" of Ohio, of which not one, according to so distinguished and well-informed an educational authority as Minister White, can rank above third or fourth class, "judged even by the American standard." The chief struggle and chief rivalry of each seems to be to obtain a larger number of students than its neighbors. One institution in Ohio has been promised a large sum of money when the number of its students attains a certain figure. The effect on entrance and other examinations is self-evident. Besides, one can not avoid reflecting that that is a rather low state of culture in which men are valued like sheep, at so much a head! To learn what a wise system of State action can do, we have but to look to Michigan, whose educational system, ending in the university at Ann Arbor, is an honor to the country.*

A third reason why there are so few college students is palpable in a literal sense — as palpable as gold and silver. The expenses of living at the first-class colleges have increased faster than the wealth of those classes which supply them with their under-graduates. A student can not live comfortably at Harvard for less than $700 per annum, but in the wealthy State of New York there are towns of several thousand inhabitants where a man can easily count on his fingers all the fathers who can educate their sons at such an expense. The scholarships at Harvard are not equal to the demand, and many who would otherwise go to Harvard are too independent to accept them. The tuition fee of $150 is comparatively enormous. The same

* For a farther consideration of this point, see the admirable address on advanced education by Dr. White.

number of hours' instruction at an expensive German university, *e. g.,* Heidelberg, do not cost one-third so much, at the
University of Geneva not one-sixth. In fact, it is cheaper to
go to Europe to study than to go to Harvard. If men of wealth
would employ their money in reducing the expensiveness of
the first-class colleges, and so opening them up to new classes
of society, they would confer a benefit on their country.

When it becomes generally understood that a college education is not a university one, but, according to the old idea,
an intellectual training which is desirable for every man who
is able to enjoy its privileges, whatever is to be his business
or profession, and when colleges return to their former aims,
often too hastily forsaken, we may expect to see classes of
the people flock to their learned halls who up to this time have
neglected them.

Universities are needed and a few of the best colleges, the
development of which already lies in that direction, ought to
supply this want. These colleges are well enough known —
Harvard, Cornell, the University of Michigan, and, since it
has been under President Barnard's management, Columbia.
Many think that Columbia has a special duty in this direction
on account of its wealth. It has also the good fortune of being
situated in a great city — the only place for a true university,
however it may be with a college. Columbia is, too, less expensive than Harvard and some other New England colleges.
In fact, in a city like New York one can live upon what he
will. Columbia's generosity in regard to tuition fees, and the
way they are remitted, is truly praiseworthy. It is said that
one-third pay none whatever; but the writer was a member of
a class in Columbia three years without learning the name of
one classmate who did not pay his tuition.

Let no one blame the presidents and professors of our best
institutions for not doing more. They are men who do not suffer morally or intellectually by comparison with the faculties
of the most renowned European universities. If they had the
same advantages as the German professors, they would not
do less in advancing science; but at present they are over-

loaded with work. They are also less independent than the German professors. Science is a tender plant, and requires favorable circumstances for a high development. A professor ought to be lifted above all fear of party and sect.

Germany has twenty-one universities, including the academy at Munster, which has the same rank. We might in the course of time support as many. Once more here is a place for government interference, for we may as well make up our minds once for all that private initiative is not sufficient. England's educational history proves it as well as America's. It is doubtful if in the whole history of the world one single case can be pointed to where private competition and private generosity have proved themselves sufficient. None but universities should be allowed to call themselves such. The government has precisely the same right to forbid this that it has to prevent me from travelling about as Mr. Evarts, and thus securing the various advantages which might accrue to me from representing myself as the Honorable Secretary of State.

The colleges could continue to give the degree of artium baccalaureus, as the French collége and lycées do; but it should be clearly understood that it is a college and not a university degree. The universities could give the artium magister, or still better, as being more distinct from the baccalaureus, the doctor philosophiae, doctor juris, doctor medicinae, doctor scientiarum naturalium, etc., as the German universities do. It should be clearly stated on the diploma in what subject the student had passed his chief examination, as is also the case in the German universities. If a student desired to teach Latin or Greek in an academy or college, he should be obliged to take a course of Latin or Greek at a university. But his doctorate of ancient classics ought not to assist him in securing a position as professor of astronomy.

5

The Idea of a University

Daniel C. Gilman

Those who watch the progress of higher education in this country are aware that a great deal of talk is current about the University, as distinguished from the College. The former term, used with caution twenty or thirty years ago at Cambridge and New Haven, is now freely employed in both places, and the ideas which it implies are recognized as important, with more or less heartiness, and more or less vagueness, all over the land. Generous gifts have been made for the establishment of university funds, and noteworthy changes have been introduced into the study-plans of the older institutions; new foundations have been laid; schemes of post-graduate work, some of them attractive and some of them repellent, have been announced in a score of places: the terms of the Master's degree have become more strict; the degree of Doctor of Philosophy has been introduced; efforts have been made to raise the standard of professional instruction in all the faculties, and the advancement of science has been favored by the establishment of astronomical observatories, laboratories of chemistry, physics, and biology, and museums of geology, archaeology, ethnology, and art.

This growth of the university idea is not restricted to any

Reprinted from *North American Review*, Vol. 133, No. 299, Oct. 1881, pp. 353-367.

region. Methods introduced into the University of Virginia, half a century ago, still exert a strong influence in the South and South-west. The universities of Michigan, Wisconsin, Minnesota, California, and of other western States, are illustrations of the popular demand for something more than a college. Successful and unsuccessful attempts to establish universities in New York, Philadelphia, Baltimore, Washington, Albany, Troy, Cincinnati, Chicago, St. Louis, and Cleveland proceed from the same aspiration. The fruitless discussion of a national university, a few years ago, indicates this desire, and so do the gifts of Cornell and Vanderbilt; while the foundation of Johns Hopkins has given an exceptional opportunity for promoting those ideas which its authorities regard as essential to a university.

It is not strange that with all this variety of effort there is some confusion of ideas, beginning with the nomenclature which still speaks of Harvard and Yale as colleges, while it designates as universities, feeble institutions scarcely known beyond the counties of their origin. The appropriate methods of work are also confounded. Students are admitted, and are even invited, to the freedom of university life, who have never pursued a collegiate course, and could not be accepted as regular students by any respectable college. Degrees lose their significance. Worse than all this, — the obligation which rests upon every scholar to advance the science which he professes is too often forgotten or neglected.

It is not so in Europe. The idea of the university is there recognized as distinct from the idea of the college. Universities are above and beyond colleges — they have prerogatives and duties which do not pertain to colleges. Their rights are rigidly protected, as their duties are clearly defined. But among Americans, a tendency to exaggerate, "to discount the future," to bestow titles by brevet, to cherish great expectations, has led enthusiastic friends of education to use the largest word in the vocabulary of pedagogics as synonymous with a word of a totally different meaning, till the confusion is so great that every writer on this subject, and every advocate of university ideas, must indicate what he considers as included in the term he employs.

There are some who consider that the chief function of a university is the bestowal of academic degrees, as in the University of London, without regard to instruction. There are others who argue that "the four faculties" (law, medicine, theology, and philosophy) must be organized for teaching; others assert that the union of all the higher educational agencies of a given region in one associated body will constitute a university. Eclectic courses and freedom of intellectual life and exertion are often spoken of as if here was the true distinction. Sometimes, "endowment for research" is advocated, as if that was the desideratum. It is not uncommon to hear that the success of a university is indicated by the number of students it brings together, or by the capital employed in university work. There are doubtless some who in their silence think that all attempt to discriminate between university and collegiate work is futile; the two names are for one thing.

All these expressions are inadequate. The idea of the university, as it seems to me, consists in the *Societas Magistrorum et Discipulorum;* an association, by authority, of Masters, who are conspicuous in ability, learning, and devotion to study, for the intellectual guidance, in many subjects, of youthful Scholars who have been prepared for the freedom of investigation by prolonged discipline in literature and science.

Institutions which perform this work must be the highest agencies employed in any community for perpetuating, advancing, and diffusing knowledge by the personal contact of teacher and pupil. They supply society with perpetual accessions of highly trained and liberally educated young men, capable of contributing to human welfare, not only in the traditional professions, but in all the complex affairs of modern life which require the application of intellectual force to difficult and often unexpected problems. Universities cannot produce intellects nor transform the weak and feeble into the strong and influential; but they can store the mind of ordinary capacity with the experience of other men; they can enlarge the

95

power of absorbing knowledge; they can discipline the faculties of memory, observation, and judgment; they can inspire the irresolute with noble aims; they can awaken the spirit of investigation and inquiry; they can show how to meet and overcome difficulties; they can prevent needless and fruitless expenditures of force; they can offer to the gifted training without which genius is commonly unfruitful. Those whom they have rightly trained may become serviceable, not merely in the pulpit, the sick-room, and the court-house, but in the school-room, the laboratory, the library, the editorial chair, the publisher's office, the halls of legislation, municipal government, civil service, the bureaus of administration and construction, the exploration of new lands, the prosecution of surveys, the conduct of great and complex industrial and commercial enterprises, and especially in the advancement of science. There is no limit to the callings to which the university may lead; there is no limit to the number of well-trained men which a thrifty young nation like ours can profitably employ,—but the overcoming of difficulties must be the work to which they have been wonted.

If this view is correct, it is obvious that libraries, observatories, and laboratories will not constitute a university unless they are attached to professional chairs. Periodicals, books, and letters sent out from a seat of learning will never take the place of living examples of study and research. It is the quality and not the number of students which will mark success. The perpetuation of what has been known is but one function of this associated work. Instruction by investigation is the keynote of university life.

Now, the organizations by which this purpose can be secured may vary very much, but it is safe to say that the idea of the university will be worked out in this country by methods which are adapted to our institutions, civil and ecclesiastical, and to our times. The American universities will have their own form—not modeled upon the English, the Scotch, or the Irish foundations, nor upon the German high-schools, in which so many young American professors have been taught, nor upon the French, Italian, or Dutch examples. The attempt to transplant or to closely imitate any one of those institutions, however excellent it may be in its place, would have but a slight chance of success. Good ideas can be derived from European universities of every type, but the American university, like the American college, and the American public school, is likely to be the product of American thought adapted to American needs and American ways. An indigenous and not an exotic plant will thrive best in our climate and on our soil. The proposition that Germans should plant a German university in this country will not probably be greeted with much favor by the citizens of either land,—nor the like proposal to found a Hebrew university. We may go farther than this, and expect that our universities will differ from one another in organization, comprehensiveness, and resources even more than the colleges. It is doubtful whether any two will be alike. There will be among us no control of a central government, as in France and Germany; no historic exemplars, as in England; no voluntary association or council of education having extended authority; and so American ingenuity, independence, indifference to conservative traditions, and love of variety will devise in different places manifold agencies and combinations of agencies for the promotion of the higher culture.

The history of our older colleges indicates in the past a healthy growth, well adapted to the new circumstances of a new country, and foretells in the near future still broader developments, in full accord with the advancement of knowledge, the increase of wealth, and the multiplication of pursuits which call for high intellectual power.

Take a conspicuous example. The institution at New Haven (well spoken of by a son of Harvard on a recent occasion as "national") was at first an idea, and that only, in the minds of Davenport, Hopkins, and other founders of the colony. After three-score years or more, the idea took the form of "a collegiate school," without at first a local habitation or a proper name. This grew to be "a college," with its fixed curriculum— a discipline of the intellect and the heart—so satisfactory as to draw pupils from every part of the land, so exemplary as to be imitated (even in minute details) by scores of more recent foundations, and so good in itself, that it would be hard to change it for something a great deal better. In the third half-century of its life, schools of professional and technical education were grafted upon the stock of what was called "the college proper," and more recently funds have been provided for the advancement of science and for the instruction of advanced scholars who are neither under-graduates nor professional students. Already there are indications that before the close of this century, the "idea of a university," which Davenport brought with him from the University of Oxford to the wilderness of Quinnipiac, having passed through the stages of the simple collegiate school, "the college proper," and the college with professional and technical schools attached to it, will have the dignity, the liberality, and the comprehensiveness of a well-endowed "university." The history of Harvard shows quite as distinctly as that just sketched how steady, vigorous, and promising has been the development of the oldest and richest of American foundations. But whatever be the form which the idea of the university assumes, whether it be developed from the collegiate germ, as at Harvard and Yale, favored by the long line of historical associations and the assured patronage of those great foundations, or be embodied in some new and unfettered organization, there are certain principles which the experience of the world seems to indicate as favorable to success.

In the first place, universities must include or must rest upon colleges. By this is meant that before a scholar is fitted for intellectual freedom, he must submit to severe and prolonged intellectual discipline. Untutored minds may think as they can and think as they like — and now and then a genius will appear among them who far transcends all ordinary thinkers, — but, as a rule, the thoughts of the untaught are of little value, because they do not know what others have thought. They sometimes produce works of imagination which delight their readers, or move them by expressions of eloquence and piety, but they seldom add to human knowledge or rise to positions of extraordinary responsibility. From the beginning of his teens, the boy who is destined to an intellectual career requires for several years to be under the watchful eye and the experienced hand of the ablest teachers whose services can be secured. He may evince more talent in one direction than in another, but he is not competent to determine what course he ought to follow. At this period it is as foolish to leave him to his own choice alone, as to send him to sea without charts and a compass. He needs an adviser all the while. Without constant help, from a prescribed curriculum or from wise counselors to whom he has easy access, he will fail to form right mental habits; he will miss the proper order of his studies, and will waste his time, force, and money.

As the world is to-day, and as it has been since the revival of letters, the boy who is destined to the life of a scholar cannot escape the early study of Mathematics, the foundation of science, and Language, the foundation of the humanities; and long before he takes up his Euclid or his Virgil he should begin the study of Nature, and learn to observe her manifold phenomena. It is not until he has acquired the elements of linguistic and scientific culture, and the principles of ethics and politics, that his mental and moral character will be matured enough for the career of a university. After this sort of training has been followed through his teens, the youth and his friends will know whether he is disposed toward higher studies, and, if so, whether he should continue to pursue the liberal arts in a department of philosophy, or should enter upon the more technical discipline of a professional school. He may now be considered as having reached the commencement of a scholar's life, and be admitted to a first academic degree. Three years or more of university study should follow his collegiate life and precede his admission to a learned profession, or to his assumption of the title of an independent teacher. During this advanced period he should be led to the investigation of old problems and new; he should master the most difficult art of using a large library, and of weighing authorities; he should raise inquiries to be determined in the laboratory; he may prepare an elaborate thesis for publication; but in all this he will still need guidance. He will require the living example of a teacher who is always learning; he must observe how the master asks and seeks to answer knotty questions; how he brings the acquisitions of past ages to bear upon problems of immediate interest never before encountered; he must try his own powers under the supervision of criticism which is both severe and friendly; and thus he may advance to a second degree in the fellowship of learning, and become, in the truest sense, a Master of Arts or a Doctor in Philosophy, Medicine, or Law.

If these remarks are correct, it is obvious that the growth of American universities is not to be promoted by the abandonment of colleges. Their courses of study will be recognized as more important than ever, because they lead to higher work. If a new university is founded, it must look for pupils among the graduates of the existing colleges, or must maintain its own collegiate staff. If an old university gives up its collegiate department, it must expect to find in the high schools and endowed academies of the country young men who are adequately prepared for university pursuits.

But at present the relations of collegiate and university work are confounded. Students rejected at the entrance examinations of an ordinary college, because they are lacking in elementary knowledge and in mental discipline, may be and are received to so-called university departments, and allowed to graduate in professional studies two years before their better-trained comrades have reached the baccalaureate. I do not remember in all the land a school of law, medicine, or divinity which demands a collegiate education or its equivalent as the condition of admission to its courses, or an examining body in any one of the three professions, or in any part of the United States, which prescribes a college training as essential to a license. We might suppose that a college diploma would by public opinion be regarded as at least necessary for the master of a high school or a grammar school, — but not even that is expected. Thus to a certain extent the university tendency has been unfavorable to colleges.

It is not surpising that, if the names of colleges and universities and the relations of their work are confounded, there should be negligence also in the bestowal of academic degrees, —not, indeed, at the best institutions, but under names and auspices which simulate responsible authority. The abuse has gone so far that within the year a manufactory of fraudulent diplomas, for which there was a European demand, has been broken up in Philadelphia by the bold and enterprising exposures of one of the newspapers. It is not easy to see how academic honors can be restored to value in this country until some reform is secured. The usage of other lands, that universities alone bestow degrees, is not the survival of a needless form; it signifies that the test and approval of scholarship shall not depend upon private instructors alone or chiefly, but that he who aspires to academic honors shall be examined and commended by those who had no part in his tutorial care. He shall win his rank in the broad arena of a university, not within the restricted walls of a college. The formula by which, in the older colleges, the president on commencement day asks the public consent of the corporation before he admits to their degrees the candidates commended by the faculty, perpetuates this idea—to which additional significance might be given by including in the board of examiners those who had taken no part in the instruction of the aspirants. In one place, the experiment has been tried of inviting professors in other institutions to set papers for the examinations in Greek, Latin, German, and French, and to give their opinions upon graduating theses; and the influence of this plan upon scholarship has been found satisfactory.

I have endeavored to give emphasis to the idea that there is a legitimate distinction between the earlier and later stages of a liberal education—the stage of discipline and the stage of guidance, the period of rules, tasks, and control, preceding the period of stimulating and quickening aspiration; but there is no doubt that both methods of training are in some degree appropriate throughout the academic life. There are likewise two sorts of professors—those who are best fitted by their patient and exact habits of intellectual action, by their well-stored memories, and by their logical modes of expression, to drill the classes over which they are placed; and there are others who have a gift for investigation, who are acute in thinking of important questions to be settled, and ingenious in devising the proper methods of solution—who delight to apply the touch-stone of truth to every doctrine, and to carry the light of modern science into fields where it has never been applied. In extremely rare cases, both sorts of power are found in one individual.

The disciplinary method of a college calls for men of high social, mental, moral, and religious character, for they are to be concerned in molding the dispositions of young men, and in forming their habits at a most critical period of life, when the parent relaxes his authority and the youth has not learned to govern himself. It requires as professors those who were born to be teachers, who delight to deal with youthful minds, to inspire them with lofty motives, to train them by the best methods, to emancipate them from the slavery of sloth, to set before them noble examples, to cherish their faith. The lessons to be inculcated during a college course include obedience to recognized authority, the performance of appointed tasks, punctuality in meeting all engagements, and the development of physical vigor, as well as the acquisition of positive knowledge and the clear expression of thought. Such discipline admits of little freedom; but restraints, if wisely adjusted, are found to be as welcome to the scholar as they are to the athlete.

University methods, assuming that the students have already received this earlier discipline, that they are in earnest in the acquisition of knowledge, and that their characters are nearly formed, require less rigid processes of education. Opportunities, advantages, assistance are freely provided, but the benefit derived from them must depend upon the individual. He may fail of his degree at the end of his course, but his daily deficiencies will not be charged against him. He may forfeit the confidence of his teachers, or even his membership in the university; he may fail to equip himself for his chosen career; but he will not be forced to learn his lesson or subjected to petty penalties. He must meet as he does in life the rewards of his own conduct. Nor will he be kept back by the neglect or dullness of his comrades. The fleetest of foot may travel as he will, without being hindered by those who are fettered.

It is clear that, while universities require as professors many good teachers, they also afford careers for minds of a different order. Men who have no skill in training youthful students, who have no sympathy with their difficulties and no patience in the requisite routine of collegiate instruction, may yet be most serviceable in the prosecution of scientific research, and very capable of giving aid to those who are already strong enough to walk alone. There is a sense in which it is true that the best of all teachers is the original investigator. His methods are not adapted to beginners. His followers may be few. But if his mind is endowed with rare qualities which have been assiduously cultivated under favorable circumstances, he will exert a powerful influence upon those who are able to follow him; he will incite his fellow teachers to constant acitivity; he will draw around him other superior minds; he will bring enduring renown to the university of which he is a member.

It is not enough that a university should have an able staff of professors, but they must have the opportunity to do the very best work of which they are capable. Leisure is one of these conditions—not idleness, nor dissipation, but that frequent release from appointed duties which brings with it repose and opportunity for unobserved work. Sever and abstract thinking demands freedom for interruption—time to gather up and reflect upon accumulated thoughts in order to perceive what new relations may be discovered among them. Writing for publication requires a great deal of labor. A scholar may be hard at work when he seems to be doing nothing; what is called absence of mind may be the opposite; it may be a separation of the intellectual faculties from the outside world, and their concentration upon ideas. The story of Newton's forgetfulness as to whether he had dined or not, often repeated of other scholars, is a natural illustration of that indifference to physical circumstances which may mark a scholar in command of all his forces, as it does a general on the field.

Service is quite as important as leisure to the scholar. He must be required to keep his armor polished and his muscles pliant. Regular duties, exacted of him in some position of responsibility, will counteract the mortal tendency to indifference and sloth, and to misdirected reflection. Of all the forms of service which a scholar can render, none tends to keep him brighter than contact with young, bright minds. Their enthusiasm, their curiosity, their ambition, will wake him up, if he is sleepy, or else desert him altogether. A company of learned men, free from responsibility as teachers, may form an academy of sciences; but they will not make a university.

The printing-press is a third requisite. Means of publication should be liberally provided for the teachers of a university, and they should be encouraged to employ this agency with freedom. It is commonly understood that the observations of an astronomer are of no value until they are published, and equally that there can be no popular sale for them when printed; but it is often forgotten that, in every department of scientific activity, the most profound and important work is of immediate interest to the smallest number of readers; and its publication must, therefore, be encouraged, not by the usual agencies of the trade, but by special funds, appropriations, and subscriptions. Indeed, a gift for the advancement of science in this country might well be directed to the establishment of a fund for the publication of original memoirs, auxiliary to that of the Smithsonian Institution, or supplementary to the funds of some of our academies. The knowing ones could tell of more than one paper kept back from the public because there are no means with which to pay the printer; of more than one valuable memoir sent abroad to be printed, because there was no place for it at home; of many that are here printed at the expense of the author. It is only when submitted to criticism that the work of a scholar is appreciated. It may be abstruse. Its practical bearings may not be apparent. It may have no value in the eyes of Philistines. But if it be honest work, in a good method, on important subjects, by a mind of acknowledged ability, it will be recognized by those who are capable of judging it.

Instruments are indispensable to the professors of a university — the latest and best which can be procured. The literary man demands his books, journals, plates, maps, as truly as the scientific man his lenses and his balances. We sometimes hear it said that hitherto there has been in this country a tendency to give disproportionate sums for the construction of buildings and the purchase of material things. This is doubtless true; yet everybody will admit that a library is more likely to be preserved and to grow if it is kept within safe walls; that the work of a chemist, a physicist, or a naturalist cannot be prosecuted without a laboratory; that collections of minerals, plants, animals, antiquities, and works of art are enhanced in value when fitly exhibited; and that residences, gymnasia, and halls of instruction and assembly are needed by every company of scholars. If the English universities are mentioned, we think of their historic towers, their spacious libraries and museums, and their well-kept grounds quite as quickly as of their Newton and Milton. It is only when buildings are in advance of the needs of an institution, or involve the use of funds required for other purposes, that their construction is to be regretted. Most of the older colleges in this country, and some of the younger, have within the last twenty years received generous gifts for buildings, and there are very few cases, if any, where the new architecture has been extravagant or unnecessary. Still, so much has been done in this way that we should now anticipate a period when gifts will be less frequently made for construction and more for the promotion of instruction and research.

In addition to leisure, duties, instruments, and means of publication, a professor needs pay. Social position he is sure to win; academic honors, in the form of titles and the membership of learned bodies, are likely to be his lot; but more substantial rewards are also his due. People are apt to forget that scholars are susceptible to the same motives as other men; money is just as useful to them as to anybody. A sense of duty, responsibility, obligation will, indeed, make them faithful; the love of knowledge will lead them to severe and protracted labor; the responses of their pupils will be a rich reward; but they are entitled to more than this—to emoluments increasing with their attainments and reputation, like those of the successful lawyer, physician, clergyman, and man of affairs. A clergyman, near Boston, referring not long ago to an increased salary which was offered him, said, in substance, "To me money means books, leisure, health, freedom from anxiety, greater power to work." That is what it means to a university professor. Intellectual force expended in writing "pot-boilers," in lecturing under adverse circumstances to winter lyceums in the country, or in undue anxiety about domestic economy, is force withdrawn from higher labors. It is bad educational economy, justified, indeed, by necessity, but not to be recommended. On the other hand, power to buy books and scientific journals for command in one's own working-room, to employ assistants, to attend literary and scientific conferences, or to visit other laboratories, collections, and countries,—such power is capital well invested and yielding income. The classical scholar who can occasionally go to Italy and Greece; the geologist and botanist who can, at his pleasure, take the field; the historian who can command the libraries of London and Paris; the astronomer who can look through other glasses and through other atmospheres than his own, has by these very opportunities, advantages which do not supersede but enhance the value of his quiet and unobserved hours of thought and study at home. The community has taken a missionary view of the college professor, and encouraged him to seek reward in the depths of his own conscience and the profounder hopes of the kingdom of heaven. It is not proved with the certainty of even probability that a missionary is any better servant of the Church when kept on spare diet, or prevented from seeking the relaxation which is essential to his health; but it is absolutely sure that a scholar cannot maintain his brightness, his enthusiasm, his susceptibility to good influences, and his fertility, if he is oppressed by anxiety as to how to pay his grocer's bills. Plant in two fields two measures of the same corn, and if you wish to be disappointed, look for your richer harvest on the thin soil of a granite hill-side, where the snows linger late in spring and the rains run rapidly off in summer.

In estimating the pecuniary returns which are due to an eminent professor, it should be borne in mind that his talents, if concentrated on the production and introduction of text-books, or devoted to technical pursuits, or to the practice of law, or medicine, or even to the pastoral charge, would be likely to reap a rich reward; and if society wishes that men of talent should forego such opportunities, equivalents must be offered. Probably no form of pecuniary aid is more encouraging to a scholar than the surety of a pension. The certainty that, if disabled by infirm health or by advancing years, he will be cared for, or, if stricken down by death in the prime of life, that his wife and children will not be penniless, is a high reward. Within a short time, two men of European reputation have declined to come to America on larger salaries than they have ever received, assigning as reasons the certainty of pensions if they remained at home.

It is obvious that universities are enormously costly. They are the product of highly civilized communities, where large sums of money can be devoted to the promotion of abstract science, and the employment of men of uncommon intellectual ability in the solution of the difficulties of mankind. There is no limit to the amount of money which they can legitimately employ, and which, as the years roll on, they will liberally repay to society by the contributions they will make to the welfare of man and to his intellectual delights. The sciences flourish best when promoted in close fellowship — cultivated, as the wheat grows, upon broad acres, and not in gardener's pots. The professors are quickened by each other's activity, are helped by each other's knowledge. Every new laboratory derives assistance from all the others, and each new department strengthens all the rest, for, on the altars of learning as elsewhere, coals blaze brighter when they touch. Nowhere is this precept more apt, — "To him that hath shall be given, and from him that hath not shall be taken away even that which he hath." The concentration of resources around a nucleus which is full of strength is the way to promote the higher education. Already the scattering of our forces among many feeble foundations called universities has retarded the advancement of knowledge and the advancement of scholarship. It is time to protest against these "will o' the wisps," which drag their followers into quagmires by the semblance of light.

Gifts bestowed upon well-established institutions are among the safest investments which can be made, either for public service or private renown, or the promotion of specific purposes. The best financial counsel of the community is usually at the service of a well-endowed college; and there is a sort of mutual assurance in the various invested funds which gives to them desirable security. Seats of learning are essentially conservative; they are slow to run risks or enter upon dangerous experiments, and their managers are usually men of probity and fidelity. Such foundations may claim to live for all time, and to be more anxious for the security of their investments than for any sudden addition to their income. As a rule, they are therefore, the best trustees which society offers for the preservation of funds.

The head of an Oxford college not long ago expressed to an American visitor his wish that all specific endowments might terminate within a very limited period — so alive was he to the awkwardness and discomfort of garbs prescribed by donors who never once thought it possible that such dresses would go out of use. Endowments for the promotion of different branches of knowledge are likely to have a more permanent value than buildings, but they should be free from all petty regulations. The liberal Californian who has just offered the sum of seventy-five thousand dollars for the endowment of a professorship in that stanch but much-buffeted institution, the State University, has set an example which may be everywhere commended, not only for the amount of his gift, but for its freedom from restrictions.

These, then, are the points to which we call attention. The

idea of the university does not depend upon the name. It makes no difference whether Yale and Harvard are called by one designation or the other; they are known to be places where university education as well as collegiate can be acquired. The glory and the activity of a university depend upon the professors. The difficulty which is now felt at home and abroad is to offer resistance to the attraction of money-making, and induce those who are fitted for advancing the highest departments of knowledge to puruse the university life. The university requires a different sort of teacher from the college, because the methods employed are essentially different. The earlier stages of a liberal culture depend on discipline; the later on inspiration. Hence, a college requires professors who love the pedagogic work, who are skilled as teachers, and who will exert a strong influence on the development of the character of their pupils; the university may be less exacting in these respects, and seek for professors whose pedagogic value will consist to a very considerable extent in their power to add to human knowledge, and the corresponding and inseparable power of interesting the highest class of youthful minds. Sometimes capacity for discipline and for inspiration will be found in the same person; but the instances are rare, and should be valued like pearls of great price. Universities cannot thrive without collegiate foundations, and must either maintain their own under-graduate departments or encourage those which are found elsewhere. Universities are so costly that but few of them can be liberally maintained in any country, and if Americans desire to see them bloom to fruitfulness among us, they must nurture well the few sturdy plants which are already growing. Thus we shall not only preserve the idea of the university but secure its reality—a place where most learned scholars and most able investigators are associated in the advancement of knowledge and the education of such youth as have been prepared by previous training for the freedom of advanced study.

6

Pettifogging Law-Schools and an Untrained Bar

David Starr Jordan

Mr. James Bryce, writing of the universities of America, uses these words: "While of all the institutions of the country they are those of which the Americans speak most modestly and indeed deprecatingly, they are those which seem to be at this very moment making the swiftest progress and to have the best promise for the future. They are supplying exactly those things which European critics have hitherto found lacking in America, and they are contributing to her political as well as to her contemplative life elements of inestimable worth."

The various influences, German, English, and American, which are moulding our higher education, are joining together to produce the American university. And the American university, as Mr. Bryce has clearly indicated, is becoming an institution in every way worthy of our great Republic. Its swaddling clothes of English tradition are being cast aside, and it is growing to be American in the high sense of adjustment to the American people's needs. The academic work of the best American institutions is characterized by vigor and thoroughness, and in the free air that pervades them there is every promise for their future.

But with all this, the professional schools of America have not taken their part in the university development. It has been

Reprinted from *The Forum*, Vol. 19, May 1895, pp. 350-355.

said of the American law-schools, for example, that "they are the weakest and therefore the worst to be found in any civilized country." Broadly speaking, and taking out some half-dozen notable exceptions (not so many nor so notable as they should be), this statement cannot be denied. Of this deficiency, its causes, and its remedy, I propose briefly to treat in this paper.

In Europe, professional training is in general the culmination of university education. It is not so in America. It is here rather a "practical short-cut" by which uneducated or ineducable men are helped to the rewards of knowledge and skill with the least possible loss of time. In most of our States, provision is made for a system of public education beginning with the common schools and culminating in the university. The law-schools, however, in the different States form no part of this system. They are rarely even in real alliance with it. Their place is with the "Independent Normal" and the "School of Oratory." Instead of a requirement of general intelligence and a special knowledge of economics, history, literature, and language, as a preparation for the study of law, our schools have been eager to admit any one who could pay the required fees and perchance read the English language.

Instead of trained professors who make the methods of investigation and instruction in law the work of a life-time, we find in most of our law-schools lawyers who have turned incidentally to teaching, with no knowledge of the methods by which teaching may be made effective. Some of them are young men who have not yet found anything more serious to do. But usually the chairs of law are occupied by broken-down lawyers, released from active practice—old men who read old lectures to audiences inattentive or occupied with newspapers, or who conduct a lifeless quiz from lifeless text-books. Sometimes able lawyers fill these chairs, men still in active practice, whose hour in the class-room is taken early in the morning or late in the afternoon, before or after the arduous duties of a day in court. With these men, the court and not the school occupies their thought and fills their ambitions.

The law students are in general assistants in law offices or clerks in business establishments. They devote their hours out-side the class-room, not to library research or to the investigations of principles and precedents, but to the making of money. The law school is expected not to interrupt their usual vocations. The atmosphere of culture which surrounds every real institution of learning, and which it is the business of great teachers to create, is unknown to the average student of law.

Often the law-school appears in its register as a branch of some university. In most such cases, this relation is one which exists only in name. It is a common expression that such and such a college is "surrounded by a fringe of professional schools." These exist as stolons or suckers around a stalk of corn, rather than as representing "the full corn in the ear." When a nominal alliance exists, it rests not often on unity of purpose or method, but on the fact of mutual service. The reputation of the university tends to advertise the law-school. The roll of law students swells the apparent attendance of the university. By the number of names on the register, the success of the American university is popularly measured.

There is, besides, a strong force of precedent which causes each new law-school to be modelled on the lines of the old ones. These influences and others oblige our universities to wink at the obvious incongruity of the requirement of elaborate and careful preparation for the study of literature, chemistry, and economics, while for the study of law a mere reading acquaintance with the English language passes as adequate. More than once, college faculties in this matter have had to subordinate their opinions to those of timid Boards of Trustees, who are afraid that high standards in a law-school would be fatal to its success, measuring success in the conventional fashion as Boards of Trustees are prone to do.

It is thus true, as President Eliot has said, that into an American law school any man "can walk from the street." But in most of the States he can do better or worse than this. From the street he can walk directly into the profession of law, disregarding even the formulae of matriculation or graduation. Even the existence of the law-school is a concession to educational tradition. It is possible with us to enter any one of the "learned professions" with no learning whatsoever. In fact, in many of our States, it requires no more preparation to be admitted to the bar than to be admitted to the sawbuck. Fortunately, admission to either on these terms carries with it no prestige or social elevation whatever. But the danger in the one case is greater than in the other. The inefficient lawyer may work the ruin of interests entrusted to him. The ignorant physician is more dangerous than the plague. The incompetent wood-sawyer harms only the wood-pile. A large part of our criminal records is devoted to legal and medical malpractice. In other words, our bulk of crime is swollen by robbery and murder committed under the guise of professional assistance. When the professions cease to be open wide to adventurers and thieves, they will rise to something of their traditional dignity. It has been said that the only "learned profession" in America at present is that of the engineer. The value of knowledge and training in the various applications of science to human affairs has always been recognized among us. The people have freely taxed themselves for industrial instruction, and it is now generally recognized as a necessary part of the State-university system. The faculty in mechanic arts stands on an equality with the university faculties, and in general the standards of admission and methods of work in these branches compare favorably with those in any other field. The reason for this is not far to seek. The necessity of education in these lines is self-evident. Men cannot trifle with the forces of nature. The incompetence, or ignorance, or dishonesty of an engineer will soon make itself evident. The incompetence of men in other professions is not less disastrous, but it is more easily concealed. And for this reason the common man regards it with greater indifference.

It seems to me that the essential weakness of the American law-school, as well as that of our professional schools in general, lies in the method of organization. They have lost their place in the university. This separation which I have tried to describe exists only in America. For this separation, the popular desire to reach these professions by short cuts, and the popular distrust of those who have done so, are equally responsible.

Our people have always been willing to tax themselves to furnish a general education for their children. The common-school idea from the very first has included a liberal education. But in most of the States, the people have at one time or another definitely refused to devote public funds to the making of lawyers and doctors. They would not, at their expense, help men into professions they believed to be overpaid as well as overcrowded. This policy has been a most shortsighted one. It has been responsible for the existence in every part of our country of hordes of pettifoggers and quacks who rob the people instead of serving them. Incompetent professional service is always robbery. The professions are overcrowded simply because they have ceased to be professions. The remedy for incompetence is found in insisting on competence. This can be done by furnishing means by which competence can be made possible.

The forces which have operated here are necessarily associated with the growth of democracy. The movement of civilization has been constantly in the direction of the extension of the powers and privileges of the few to the many. By this influence, careers and distinctions once reserved for the aristocracy have been opened to the common man. One immediate result, temporary no doubt, is that the common man has invaded these provinces without abating one whit of his commonness. This is a necessary phase of the vulgarization which follows the extension of justice known as democracy. It is connected with the vulgarization of the press, the theatre, the pulpit, which must follow their adjustment to the needs of the many rather than to the finer tastes or juster judgment of the few. The common man is satisfied with common lawyers. When he ceases to be thus satisfied, he is no longer common. That his freedom of choice and the training which results from it will in the long run eliminate this vulgarization, is the justification for democracy. Our hope for the future lies largely in our recognition of the badness of the present. From the weakness of our professional schools, the common man is the chief sufferer. And already he is joining in the demand that these schools be made better. It is absolutely certain that those schools whose work is most thorough and whose requirements are most exacting will have the most students, as well as the best ones. It is not true that the students of America demand poor instruction because it is cheap.

Notwithstanding all adverse conditions, there have been many great teachers of law in America. The great teacher makes his influence felt, whatever the defects in the organization of the institution which claims his services. The present prominence of the University of Michigan rests in large degree on the work of Thomas M. Cooley. The work of John B. Minor in the University of Virginia gives a well-deserved prominence to the Virginia school of law. Other law professors have added in no small degree to the prestige of Harvard, Columbia, Cornell, and the University of Pennsylvania. In all these institutions, a strenuous effort has been made to place the work in law on a basis not less high than that occupied by history and economics. In other words, in these and in some other institutions, it is only a question of a short time till the law faculty shall be made not an "annex," but an integral part of the faculty of the university. When this is done, the requirements for graduation as a lawyer will not be less than equivalent to the work for which a degree would be granted to a chemist or a civil engineer.

To find the cause of any deficiency is to go a long way toward curing it. In this case, it seems to me, the remedy lies in placing the instruction in law on the same footing as that of other departments of the university. The teaching of law should be a life-work in itself. The requirements and methods in law should be abreast of the best work in any department. The university atmosphere and the university ideals should surround the student in law as well as the student in history. No one should be encouraged to take professional studies until he is capable of carrying them on seriously and successfully. There is, moreover, no reason for segregating the teachers of law in any way from the other members of the university faculty. As well make chemistry or economics a separate school as to set off the law by itself. All these separations may be made in name, but they should not exist in fact. The elements of law have as strong claim to a place in general education as the elements of geometry or psychology. Even for purposes of professional education, it is better that the study of law should be carried on simultaneously with that of the historical and social sciences, which are its natural associates. The basis of law is in the nature of man, not in the statutes of the United States nor in those of England. The common law has its source in man and his civilization, not in the books. This the student must learn to know and feel. So history, social science, and law must be mutually dependent on one another. The student of the one cannot be ignorant of the others. The suggestion that social studies should accompany rather than precede law studies has lately received the strong advocacy of Dr. Woodrow Wilson. This association should give to the student not only a lawyer's training but a scholar's horizon. Without this, broad views in jurisprudence and in politics are impossible. Such a course of study would give dignity to the general culture of the college. A student takes a better hold on culture-studies where they are clearly related to the work of his life.

Moreover, the politicians of each country are, for the most part, its lawyers. Our lawyers are our rulers. We can never hope to see our States well governed till its lawyers are well trained. There can be no political conscience except as an outcome of political knowledge. Right acting can come only as a result of right thinking. The men who think right will in the long run act in accord with their knowledge. Those who have known that there is a science of human institutions can never wholly forget that fact. There can be no right thinking in matters of public administration without a knowledge of the laws of growth of human institutions. Only in accordance with these laws is good government possible. Of these fundamental laws of being the statutes of man must be an expression. Where they are not so, the people have sooner or later a fearful score to pay. The Fates charge compound interest on every human blunder, and they have their own way at the last.

Section II

Administrative Aspects

7

The State University in America

George E. Howard

Higher education has long been growing more rational. Yet
there is a widespread feeling of discontent with the present
ideal of academic culture which sometimes degenerates into
downright pessimism. It must be conceded that education
costs too much time and too much money for the kind. The
college curriculum should be still further transformed in order
to bring it into harmony with the requirements of modern life.
Our average standard of attainment is very low, and the
reason is plain, — we have wasted our resources. But happily
we are ceasing to be proud of the fact that we have "four hundred colleges and universities." With us, as in England, the
conviction is deepening that the founding of a college is not
necessarily a blessing to the community. Accordingly, the two
most recent proposals for university reform have had in view
a shortening of the undergraduate course to facilitate an earlier
entrance on the professions, and a general elevation of the
standard of culture for the whole country through a proper
division of labor. The earnest discussion drawn out by President Eliot's recommendation to reduce the course of Harvard
to three years has called attention to the arbitrary barriers
still set up between the so-called "disciplinary" and the professional studies; while President White's suggestive plan for

Reprinted from *Atlantic Monthly*, Vol. 67, No. 401, March 1891,
pp. 332-342.

relegating most of our colleges to the rank of gymnasia, intermediate between the public schools and a small group of real
universities, places before us in unmistakable terms the waste-
fulness and the inherent vices of petty endowments, — the imperative need of large revenues in order to meet the demands
of modern science. But in its details Dr. White's classification
is impracticable, it seems to me, because it ignores organic and
historical differences in the character of American schools.
The smaller colleges and the smaller universities, whether
sectarian or secular, whether resting on private endowments
or created and supported by the State, will in due time, it is
hoped, through a process of evolution, directed by "right
reason" and wise "educational effort," take their places in the
lower rank assigned them in this scheme. The differentiation
of a class or classes of real universities as opposed to a more
numerous body of intermediate colleges, frankly acknowledg-
ing themselves to be such, will indeed, there is reason to believe, be the result of social evolution. But that evolution must
necessarily express, not ignore, the deeper lines of historical
development. It must have as its vital principle a powerful
social idea, a national sentiment. Now, as a matter of fact, is
not such an evolution really in process, — an evolution whose
roots are in past generations, which is sustained by national
policy, and which needs only more conscious direction to enable it to produce the requisite concentration and a standard
of academic culture which shall at any rate prove satisfactory
to the people? Such an evolution may be seen, I think, in the
rise of a close relation between the State and higher education.
I venture to suggest that any hopeful plan for a division of
labor among collegiate institutions must begin with the state
universities. Even the oldest of these have had but a brief
experience; yet so uniform and rapid has been their development that already two facts are plainly revealed: first, the
state university is the latest and noblest product of the same
tendency in American thought which has produced the common school; secondly, through its novel and close relation to
the State, it has differentiated a distinct organism and a distinct

character which entitle it to be regarded as the American type.
These propositions will now be discussed in the order named.

I. The rise of a national sentiment and a national policy in
favor of the public support of lower education preceded and
prepared the way for a like development in case of the higher,
and therefore it will be first noticed. The genesis of the American free school system must be sought in the early town records of New England. In the old home, popular education
had been looked upon as the proper function of the clergy
aided by private benevolence. Neither public nor local taxation was thought of for this purpose. In the New World, the
conception of the proper sphere of local and state action was
broadened. Just as the celebration of marriage was handed
over to the justice of the peace and the probate of wills to the
county court, so the supervision of primary and secondary
education was taken from the church and vested in the civil
community. Before the middle of the seventeenth century the
Massachusetts towns were supporting free schools by local
rates voted by themselves, and long before the Revolution
primary education had been made practically compulsory
throughout the greater part of New England. An ordinance of
the Dorchester town meeting in 1645 contains all the essential
features of our present school district organization. In 1647,
the General Court of Massachusetts required every town of
fifty families to establish elementary schools; and soon after
grammar schools were provided for in larger towns. A great
epoch in the history of social progress was thus made when our
New England ancestors recognized the support of popular
education as the proper function of local government. The
introduction of the school rate as a legitimate item of public
taxation deserves a memorable place in American annals. The
event is all the more remarkable because it anticipated the
development of thought in the mother country by two centuries
and a half; for, on account of religious strife and the dread of
secularizing education, it was not until 1890 that a general
system of free public schools was established in England. Our
forefathers, it is true, in this instance, as on some other oc-

casions, builded more wisely than they knew. It was probably
not imagined, in 1647, that public education was really being
taken out of the hands of the church. Indeed, the primary
motive of the Massachusetts statute of that year was to promote religious knowledge, — to circumvent the wiles of "yt
ould deluder Satan," and prevent the true sense of Scripture
from being "clouded by false glosses of saint seeming de-
ceivers." But before the Revolution the theory of state support
of popular education was consciously accepted, with a good
understanding of its inevitable consequences. It is difficult
to exaggerate the gift of New England to the American people;
for though elsewhere, in the middle colonies and in the South,
free public schools were planted, and sometimes were encouraged by legislation, to the New England colonies chiefly
is due the honor of having created an American system of
secular common schools, and of having fostered into vigorous
life the American political sentiment that the State should
educate her children as a safeguard to herself. With the adoption of the Ordinance of 1787 this idea found expression as a
distinct policy, which has been acted on consistently ever
since. Not only does the compact declare that in the territory
northwest of the Ohio "schools and the means of education
shall forever be encouraged;" but already in the Ordinance of
1785, for the survey and sale of Western lands, it had been
provided that lot number sixteen in every township should be
reserved for the support of public schools. A similar provision
was made in the grant to the Ohio Company in 1787. Here
also Congress, like the Puritans of 1647, did not fully appreciate the importance of its acts. Dr. Knight has shown that the
gift of Congress "was not made with the sole thought of promoting education," but rather was wrung from it, as a necessary inducement to customers in the sale of Western lands.
Nevertheless, a national policy was established. Every State
since admitted into the Union has received one or two sections
in each township for the support of common schools. Thus the
national government joins hands with the State, and the State
with the local communities, in the support of popular educa-

tion. The common school as a political institution is already thoroughly affiliated with other members of the social body. It no longer sustains merely a relation to the social organism; it has become a part of it. It is a township in miniature, whose meeting votes taxes and makes by-laws as naturally as does the town meeting itself. Apparently, it is nearly as well grounded as if, like the township, its roots were planted in the ancient German forest. So firmly has the idea of a completely secularized public school laid hold of popular sentiment that any sectarian attack upon it is sure to call forth general and indignant resistance, as an assault on one of the most sacred of American principles.

The secularization of higher education has been a matter of much slower growth, and the causes are not far to seek. In method, organism, and sometimes in spirit, the foundations of the colonial era were reproductions of Cambridge or Oxford colleges. The principal defects of the English system were perpetuated. The English universities were modeled directly upon the University of Paris, and therefore were dominated by monastic traditions. They were state institutions placed in subordination to a church establishment. Most of the early American colleges were intended practically to be the same. In fact, if not always in theory, they represented the union of church and state. They were created primarily to provide a learned ministry, and next for the general public good. The idea of the age is well expressed in the charter of Yale, whose foundation was entrusted by the Assembly to ten "reverent ministers of the gospell" who, out of their "zeal for the upholding and propagating of the Christian protestant religion, by a succession of learned and orthodox men," had petitioned for the establishment of a school in which youth may be "fitted for publick imployments both in church and civill state." Thus the ecclesiastical tradition, though weakened, entered into the life of the American college, — the idea of a necessarily close relationship between the professorial and the priestly office; and this tradition has been very difficult to overcome. The narrow sphere assigned to higher education in the early college is also a part of our English heritage. Divinity, mathematics, and the dead languages — the principal elements of the traditional "classic" course, until a few years since the only honorable part of our curriculum — were the chief subjects of study. A premium was put upon the acquisition of Latin and Greek at the expense of the mother tongue. In short, from the English universities of the seventeenth century — then just entering upon that era of decline which reached its lowest point in the time of Gibbon and Adam Smith — we have inherited that mediaeval spirit which has prevented our schools from entering into their proper relations to society. Still, the germs of our present system of state schools were planted in the colonial period. In nearly every instance the college was aided by the legislature, through taxation, exemption, grants of land, and appropriations of money. Harvard, in particular, was in all these ways drawn into close connection with the State. Indeed, before the Revolution, she appears to represent the nearest approach to the modern idea of a state college. Fortunately, also, her charter was surprisingly liberal. It contained neither sectarianism nor dogma. By it the college was not placed in dependence on the Puritan clergy. So that Harvard, without violating the letter of her charter, has at last become a foremost leader in the secularization of American culture; and in these days, naturally enough, like the state university, she has to endure the assaults of sectarianism on the alleged ground of irreligion.

The colonial era was therefore a time of preparation; but the conception of the completely secularized state university did not yet exist. Its rise was made certain by that event, so full of significance for the entire institutional history of this country, to which I have already referred, the adoption of the Ordinance of 1787. Ten days after that instrument had declared the encouragement of education to be a public trust, two townships were reserved by Congress, in the grant to the Ohio Company, for the endowment of a "literary institution," to be applied to the intended object by the legislature of the State. Soon after, a third township was set apart for a similar purpose in the Symmes tract. Thus was the first step taken in the development of a national policy. Tennessee and every State admitted into the Union since 1800, except Maine and West Virginia, which had no public lands, and Texas, which was abundantly able to take care of herself, have received two or more townships for the endowment of higher education. To these so-called "seminary" grants many flourishing institutions owe their origin.

A second and more important step was taken in 1862. By the Morrill act of that year, one of the noblest monuments of American statesmanship, every State is given thirty thousand acres of land "in place," or its equivalent in "scrip," for each of its Senators and Representatives in Congress, for the purpose of endowing "at least one college, where the leading object shall be, without excluding other scientific and classical studies, and including military tactics, to teach such branches of learning as are related to agriculture and the mechanic arts, . . . in order to promote the liberal and practical education of the industrial classes in the several pursuits and professions of life." Here the central thought is utility, to do something for society which the existing colleges are not doing. In his own words, the fundamental idea of Senator Morrill was to assist "those much needing higher education for the world's business." This magnificent gift has been the means of aiding about fifty colleges and universities; and of these, according to Professor Blackmar, at least thirty-three were called into existence by it. Moreover, it is strong evidence that the educational policy of the national government is gaining popular sanction that Congress has felt justified in supplementing the gift of 1862 by two later endowments. The Hatch bill of 1887 gives to each State fifteen thousand dollars a year, for the purpose of establishing "experiment stations" in connection with the colleges of agriculture and the mechanic arts; and the act is especially noteworthy as a legislative attempt on a wide scale to render science useful to the people. Already many stations have been organized and much good work has been done. Thus, not only is an organized host of trained scientists led to extend helping hands to every branch of agricultural industry, but the influence of all this new activity on the general academic life is stimulating in a high degree. Finally, by the Morrill act of 1890, each State is granted an additional sum of fifteen thousand dollars, to be increased until the annual amount reaches twenty-five thousand dollars, to further the general educational objects of the endowment of 1862.

Here, then, is a fact of the greatest historical significance. Almost before society is aware of it there has come into existence an American system of public universities, at once the complement and the crown of an American system of public schools. In its creation, as in the creation of the latter, the State has joined hands with the nation. The gifts of Congress have been administered solely by the State, which, be it well noted, has supplemented them by liberal taxation and generous appropriations. In the West and Southwest, which have profited both by the seminary and agricultural grants, the state university is already the great educational fact, the educational heart, of the community. In its history, if I read the signs of the times aright, is involved the history of higher education in the United States.

II. If we now fix our eyes on the six or eight foremost schools of the Northwest, whose development has been guided mainly by the University of Michigan, — not forgetting that some of our best institutions elsewhere, from Vermont to the Carolinas, are state schools, — we shall see that the differentiation of the state university has been determined by its peculiar relation to society. Governed usually by a board of regents, whose members are either appointed by the governor or elected by popular vote, organized under the laws of the State, often dependent on the legislature for present means of support, it touches the general body politic at every point, and its pulse beats in sympathy under every influence which affects the commonwealth for good or ill. It is in an important sense itself a political body, and in this fact lies its permanent strength, and sometimes its temporary weakness. Thus its growth has been retarded by a lack of public sympathy. In

1787 it was the zeal of Pickering, Cutler, and their associates which forced the adoption of the new educational policy upon a reluctant Congress. Thought was in process of transition. It was dimly forseen that the proposed seminaries must be secular schools; hence, in the case of Ohio, religion received a separate endowment; and even this experiment was not repeated. But the growth of a popular sentiment in favor of the state university was long hindered by two powerful forces. One was the tradition that religious instruction ought always to constitute an essential part of higher education; and this idea was not weakened by the dread of rivalry on the part of the private colleges. A second influence was the belief, also a survival, that higher education is a luxury for wealth and leisure to enjoy, not a necessity of life for the industrial and political callings. There are still men of culture and liberal views, warm friends of the free school, who are opposed, on principle, to the public maintenance of higher education. The writer has known the support of the state university to be seriously imperiled, and even its accumulated revenue partially withheld, on this ground; with how little justification will, it is hoped, presently be made clear. Public apathy and lack of foresight have had their worst consequences in the management of the "seminary" lands. The pitiful tale has been twice told, and need not be repeated. Suffice it to say that Ohio, after a century, receives from her sixty-nine thousand acres the wretched pittance of some thirteen thousand dollars a year. Indiana has fared a little better. Illinois simply flung her lands away at one dollar and a quarter an acre, and then for nearly thirty years her legislature misappropriated the slender income of the fund to other uses in order to decrease taxation. In this case, at least, the jealousy of private colleges was in part responsible for the selfish course pursued. Wisconsin has been the rival of Illinois in bad management. Her endowment was squandered chiefly as an inducement to immigration. It reveals the state of public sentiment that some of her lands were offered by the legislature at a less minimum price than that for which the common school lands at the same time were

129

sold. Even those States which, like Michigan, Minnesota, and Nebraska, have been most prudent in the management of their endowments have come far short of an ideal policy; and this applies also to the grant of 1862. Everywhere the heritage of posterity has been discounted. Wherever practicable, all college lands remaining unsold should at once be taken from the market and leased, subject to reappraisement at short intervals. Moreover, a second serious error has been committed. In several cases, instead of using the proceeds of all the government grants for the endowment of one institution, two or more schools have been established. This is a wasteful policy, a repetition of the disastrous blunder of the religious denominations. The income from all the national gifts, however liberally supplemented by taxation and special appropriations, can never become a dollar too much for the support of one real university. Other things being equal, those States which, like Nebraska, Minnesota, and Wisconsin, have centralized their resources in the upbuilding of a single institution have the most prosperous future before them.

It was inevitable that the state university, like the public school, should become thoroughly secularized. Formal religious instruction has no place in an institution supported by general taxation. Yet a principle which seems so clear to the impartial judgment and so entirely in harmony with American ideas has been by no means silently admitted. On the contrary, in more than one instance its acceptance has been gained only after years of bitter controversy, and then under protest. In fact, the state university is still assailed by sectarianism with stock charges of irreligion and immorality. Nevertheless, it is evident that Christian influences prevail in the academic life. Probably in every faculty the great majority of the instructors are church members; and they are often acknowledged leaders in the work of their respective denominations. Active Christian associations are everywhere maintained by the young men and women. In Ann Arbor, guilds for "religious and social culture," composed chiefly of university students, have been organized within the various churches. Theoretically it seems clear that the moral tone of the state university will remain in harmony with that of a society whose cardinal principle is entire separation of church and state. There must be full toleration. Hence religious tests in appointments have been abandoned by the foremost institutions. There are thoughtful men who believe that the moral atmosphere has become purer as the secularization has become more complete. Various influences, however, have coöperated to this end. No competent observer can doubt for an instant that the modern revolution in academic methods has effected a revolution for good in academic morality. Manliness, sincerity, and conscientiousness are the legitimate fruits of the present way of "teaching by investigation." The spirit of comparative science is more likely to foster honesty and truthfulness than is a regimen of conduct, and the laboratory is the best academic police system ever invented. Beyond question, the state university is a great moral power in the community. Nay, though the statement may prove startling to some, she tends in various ways to exert a salutary influence on the denominational schools. As she grows in strength and prestige her methods are imitated, and she becomes a standing rebuke to show and pretense, the vices to which the weaker colleges are particularly exposed, and to which they sometimes succumb.

But there are certain features of her policy which may have much to do with determining the moral character of the state university. Of these the most important is coeducation. It was perhaps to be expected in the democratic West that women should enjoy the same privileges as men in schools sustained by the public bounty. Yet it was not until 1870 that the University of Michigan ventured to open her doors to both sexes on equal terms. Her example has been followed by every state university in the West, and by most of the denominational schools. It would doubtless be rash, at so early a day, to predict the ultimate consequences of coeducation. It may, however, be stated that, in the opinion of almost every Western educator qualified by experience to form a judgment, its present results are good, and it is likely to remain a permanent element of public education.

Finally, it may be mentioned that the dormitory does not generally flourish in connection with the state universities. With the abandonment of this survival of the ancient English "halls" and "hostels," the problem of discipline is greatly simplified. Hazing and vandalism are seldom seen in the West. There is little dissipation. The student, while devoting himself mainly to the special objects of his academic life, remains a member of the social body. He strives to put away childish things, and does not forget that his chief business is to prepare himself for the performance of social duty. He learns that the best way to fit himself for active life is to remain a part of it. There really does not appear to be any good reason for lamenting the decay of those much-lauded associations which college life in community is said to foster. With that other fond superstition, "class spirit," let this one also be relegated speedily to its proper place among the traditions of the past; for is not the development of a healthy civic sentiment a far nobler object of university education? It may prove also that the weakening of the somewhat artificial bond of the class leads to the strengthening of those more natural affiliations which exist wherever there is a freer commonalty.

In the evolution of her educational policy, the state university has from the very beginning looked to Germany for guidance. Only in that nation did there exist a state system of higher education which could be studied with profit. By a fortunate circumstance, the University of Michigan was brought directly under the influence of German ideas at the time of her organization, in 1837, through the adoption by the legislature of a report of Mr. J. D. Pierce, superintendent of public instruction, who had made a careful study of the Prussian schools. But there has been no servile imitation. Outwardly, the state university, with its group of separately organized schools, colleges, or departments, each comprising a constantly increasing number of parallel courses, follows in broad outline the German model. German methods have been adapted to American conditions, while the vitalizing influence of the free spirit of German inquiry is a safe guarantee that a worthy standard of culture will be attained. Indeed, the rapid growth of some, even of the younger, state universities in recent years is very largely due to the extraordinary number of their professors who have received their training at Leipzig, Berlin, or some sister school. Nevertheless, the founding of a state university has usually been no easy task. The problem of administration, in particular, has often, in the formative period, been the source of much misdirected effort and unseemly strife. Briefly stated, the fundamental reason therefor is failure to appreciate the really public character of such an institution. Very naturally, the influence of the old denominational college, with its narrow range of prescribed studies and its ecclesiastical traditions, has perpetuated itself in the faculties and governing bodies. Modern science and specialization have come tardily, under pressure of public criticism. Slowly it has become clear that the state university professor holds a novel position. He stands in full view of a public which pays his salary, and is therefore little disposed to show indulgence for pedantry or incapacity. To be really successful, he must be a man of broad sympathies and lofty ideals; he must keep in touch with humanity.

The state university cannot be said to have been very fortunate in the matter of the chief executive. Many a man of culture and good intentions has failed in the president's chair, because he has been unable to rid himself of old ideals and adapt himself to new conditions. It has been impossible for him to perceive that, in a state university, professor, president, and regent hold each a public office which must be recognized. Hence he has played the part of "universal doctor," which is incompatible with modern specialization, and leads to insincerity; or that of autocrat, which is an encroachment on the functions both of faculty and regents, and leads to revolution. Public sentiment in the West seems to favor a strong executive. But the old notion that the president should be "chief educator" is happily passing away. It is beginning to be realized that what is needed in the executive, at any rate in the present phase of state universities, is not profound learning, but administrative skill and capacity for public affairs. In short, the office of university president is becoming a business profession, in which only he who is specially fitted for it by nature or by training need hope for success. The University of Michigan has had her full share of trouble, but the remarkable development of the last twenty years is owing largely to the fact that she has had at the helm a man able to grasp the idea of the American state university. Under his guidance the institution has kept pace with social progress. To her is due in no small measure the liberalization of higher education in the United States. She has been a pioneer in various important reforms which have eventually found their way into other Western schools, sometimes into those beyond the Alleghanies; and during the past two decades has been developed the system of accredited high schools, by which students are admitted to the University on diploma. This has already been carried from Michigan into several other States; and it is a fact of great historical interest, for thus the American public school and the American public university have joined hands. In consequence, the latter is already taking deeper hold on the affections of the people; and this result seems likely to be furthered by the movement for "university extension," already promising so well in Wisconsin.

One important element of a real university is inherent in the very nature of a university supported by the State; she must, when fully developed, aim at the *universitas* of knowledge; for her curriculum must satisfy the demands of a complex and progressive society, whose creature she is. First of all, a helping hand must be extended to the industries. The natural and physical sciences hold, and must continue to hold, a very high place in the academic life. Costly laboratories filled with expensive appliances are rapidly appearing. These challenge public appreciation, and money therefor is freely supplied. Nor are studies sometimes regarded as less practical neglected. Classical and modern philology have found a congenial home

134

in the West. Sanskrit has gained zealous votaries beyond the Missouri. There, also, a laboratory of psycho-physics has just been erected by a disciple of Wundt. Colleges of medicine and law are likewise coming in response to popular demand. For in few things is the State more deeply concerned than in the growth of medical science; and in an age of social revolution, when every part of our legal and constitutional system is being probed to the bottom, when legislation is resorted to more and more as a heal-all for every public ill, real or imaginary, the State surely has urgent need of an educated bar as a safeguard to herself.

But in no way does the state university discharge her public trust more faithfully than in the study of those questions which directly concern the life and structure of our social organization. Administration, finance, constitutional history, constitutional law, comparative politics, railroad problems, corporations, forestry, charities, statistics, political economy, — a crowd of topics, many of which, a few years ago, were unheard of in the schools, are being subjected to scientific treatment. Unless I greatly misapprehend the nature of the crisis which our nation has reached, it is in the absolute necessity of providing the means of instruction in these branches that we may find a very strong, if not unanswerable, argument in favor of the public support of higher education. The bare statement of several well-known facts will enable us to understand the crisis of which I speak.

We have fairly entered upon the third great phase of our national development. The first phase closed with the Revolutionary War and the birth of the nation. The second was the creation and settlement of the Constitution, terminating with the civil war and the reëstablishment of self-government in the South. During this period our material resources were explored, population and wealth increased, and society became complex. We now find ourselves face to face with the momentous and difficult questions of administration. Henceforth the State must concern herself with the economics of government and with the pathology of the social organism. The fact is that in the science of administration, municipal, state, or central, we are as a nation notoriously ignorant. Beguiled by the abundance of our resources, we have allowed ourselves to become awkward and wasteful in nearly every department. But the growing discontent and misery of the people admonish us that the time for reform has come. Hereafter taxation and finance, the tariff and corporations, labor and capital, social evils and the civil service, must absorb the attention of statesmen. Now, all these things are precisely the problems which can be solved successfully only by specialists. No amount of experience or general information will enable the legislator who does not know how to gather and classify social and economic facts, or at least who does not comprehend the nature of the evidence afforded by such facts, to frame wise or even safe laws on these subjects. In future, only men carefully trained in the schools can safely be placed at the head of state departments. Yet as a matter of fact the ignorance of the average American law-maker in statistical, administrative, economic, and political science is incredibly profound. How really formidable is the danger which threatens us on account of unskillful tinkering with the delicate mechanism of society we cannot fail in some measure to appreciate when we reflect that the biennial volume of legislative enactments is constantly being enlarged; while at the same time a greater and greater portion of such enactments relates to what has hitherto been regarded as the proper sphere of individual liberty, to the most complex interests of commerce and other industries. Undoubtedly there is a growing tendency, for good or ill, to extend the domain of state interference and regulation. The State, therefore, has urgent need of citizens carefully trained in the science of politics. If she be justified in the maintenance of common schools, in order that every man may be fitted for the intelligent use of the ballot, she is also justified in the support of higher education, for her very existence may depend upon it. This may prove to be the safeguard of our republic. Indeed, it would seem that the statesmanship of the future must proceed from the school of political science. To study society itself, to afford the most ample means for the acquirement of a thoroughly scientific political education in every department, is the primary duty, the highest office, of the state university.

Such, then, is the tendency of American public education. Surely the outlook is full of promise. I do not believe that in the end the ideal of culture will be lowered by a too fierce utilitarianism. True, a new standard of culture may be established, one which shall adjust itself from generation to generation, according to the conceptions of an advancing civilization; and a new definition of culture may be constructed, one which shall embrace the industries and the mechanic arts. This will be well. It is no longer safe to set up an aristocracy of studies. From Germany even now comes the cry of over-education. An "educated proletariat," we are assured, is seriously threatening the security of the State. It behooves us well to heed the warning.

It seems probable, from what has been said, that the work of higher education in this country will in future be divided among three classes of institutions whose differentiation is well under way. From a national point of view, the group of state universities appears to be most important; for eventually nearly every new State, as well as some of the original thirteen, will have a university which, as a rule, will outrank every other school within its borders. Here there can be no fixed or arbitrary standard of admission. The opportunities for continuation of study may indeed be very large; but the state university must begin where the average high school leaves off. There will also be a small group of richly endowed private foundations, situated principally in the older States. For these the minimum requirement may safely remain very high; and, from present indications, they will tend more and more to restrict their activity to graduate instruction. They will offer the best opportunity for specialization and the pursuit of culture for its own sake. There remains the formidable body of denominational colleges, having for the most part very slender resources, and consequently a very low average standard of attainment. For this class centralization is urgently needed;

and it seems as if it were likely to be realized through the sharp rivalry of the universities. The first result of that rivalry is very suggestive. The denominational schools are themselves becoming secularized. The appointment of a layman as president of Amherst, of another as president of the Northwestern University at Evanston, and the choice of laymen as trustees of the new Baptist University of Chicago have recently attracted public attention as striking illustrations of this fact. Again, it is unquestionably true that leading churchmen are more keenly alive than ever before to the need of consolidation. There are indications of a movement in this direction which may become general. Already in some instances weak colleges have been discontinued, in order to build up strong central institutions. Without doubt these tendencies will receive the hearty encouragement of all thoughtful men. So it may happen in time that we shall have a class of good intermediate colleges; while many foundations now bearing the name of college or university may be abolished, or relegated to the rank of training schools.

8

University Administration

W. T. Hewett

The methods of university government have occasioned little discussion in this country. The theory of education, the order of studies, the relative value of classical and scientific training, the relation of general and professional studies in academic instruction, have been considered, but the form of the constitution by which a university is administered has not seemed worthy of equal regard. The voluntary character of most of our higher institutions of learning, founded as they are by private beneficence, and independent of state control, has protected their organization from public criticism. As private corporations, existing by a special charter, they have been free from legislative inquiry, and only remotely subject to popular judgment. Varied as their constitution is, it has been tacitly assumed that the mode of their government accomplishes satisfactory, if not the highest results. This diversity of administration implies that one system meets the requirements of modern learning as well as another, or that the mode of university organization is a matter of indifference, instead of demanding the profoundest study and the most thoughtful examination of the results attained in the past, and comparison with the university systems of Europe, where a longer experi-

Reprinted from *Atlantic Monthly*, Vol. 50, No. 300, Oct. 1882, pp. 505-518.

ence has been had in dealing with the problems of advanced education.

Many vital questions connected with university organization in this country still remain unsettled; the experience of two hundred years has contributed no general policy or established views. A period of empiricism too frequently attends the institution of a new university or the inauguration of a new administration. Were a university a private enterprise, with no responsibility to the nation as a whole, and with no further interests affected than those of the owner, we could look with greater equanimity upon the tentative methods and immense waste of resources that too often accompany its foundation. But the loss is far greater, from another stand-point: unscientific administration cripples the cause of sound learning, misdirects honest effort; and those who teach and those who receive instruction suffer the consequences of arbitrary methods and a superficial philosophy. The world has been at school for eight hundred years in university administration, and the human mind still longer as regards the process of its growth and development; but every new American institution begins from the beginning to settle its own principles of government and forms of instruction. It cannot be seriously maintained that the highest results have been achieved through these various systems; even the most successful university shows the possibility of advance, and it is well to consider the defects of the present system.

The questions of university organization may be divided into two classes: those relating to the external government, and those affecting the internal administration. First as to the external government. The charter is usually bestowed upon certain specified corporators, in whom the property is vested, who possess the power to determine the general character of the university, to enact all needed laws for its government, and to choose their own successors. The board is thus an independent, self-perpetuating body, possessing a wide jurisdiction, and free from accountability to any revisory power. In New England, however, there are in several colleges two

governing bodies, called by various names, as the "Corporation and Overseers," the "Trustees and Overseers," the mutual rights of which are not always clearly specified, but where one body practically originates action, and the other retains a power of revision and veto.

There is a different method of government in certain universities founded by states and municipalities. The board of regents of the University of Michigan is nominated by political conventions and elected by a popular vote; the University of Wisconsin is ruled by regents, appointed by the governor from each congressional district. The equal rights of all sections of the state are thus secured, but the trustees are necessarily removed from the vicinity of the university, and consequently have a limited personal acquaintance with the needs of the institution entrusted to their care. In some cases the relation of the college or university to the state is extremely close, and it becomes a permanent *protégé,* often supported by an annual grant. Many of these state universities lead a stormy existence amid the strife of parties. In universities founded by cities, the trustees are sometimes elected by the city government, or appointed by the mayor, and their history partakes of the vicissitudes of city politics. Universities established by religious denominations sustain a particular relation to a bishop or church, and in some cases the trustees are elected by religious conferences.

These different systems are alike in entrusting the oversight of the interests of a university to a body of men outside of same. Nothing analogous to this is found abroad, save perhaps in some English schools; as a feature of university government in England, France, or Germany, it cannot be said to exist. It is therefore a purely American institution, and must be defended as meeting better than anything else the wants of the nation, and therefore worthy of preservation, or as having a right to exist because nothing better has been devised to take its place. The whole question demands the most serious consideration, for upon its right decision the highest development of our educational institutions depends, as well as the future

position which this country shall hold in promoting the advance of learning. To our universities we must look for all intellectual training for the professions, as well as for all research which shall contribute to the progress of science.

The present organization of American colleges has changed in some important particulars from the form of government originally introduced. The first scholars of this country had been educated in the universities of Europe: most had graduated at Oxford or Cambridge, or studied at Edinburgh or Utrecht, or Leiden. The early constitution of the college was modeled after that of the English universities.

Harvard University presents certain points of resemblance to the system of the English colleges. By the charter of 1650, which is still in force, the president and fellows of Harvard College became a body corporate, enjoying the right of administering the funds and making all rules for the government of the college, as well as of electing their successors in office. The former board of overseers was retained, embracing the governor, the deputy governor, and the leading clergymen and magistrates of the adjoining towns. This double organization was designed to perpetuate in the government of the college the close relation of church and state to all educational institutions. The overseers had been the sole governing board, but, as constituted, it was not found equal to the functions which devolved upon it. Many of the members resided at a distance, and few could have an immediate knowledge of the needs of the college and an insight into its workings. Differences in religious belief also divided the colony, and introduced bitterness and strife in the election of members of the board and in the choice of the president and tutors, which continued even after later modifications of the charter. The state retained an unfavorable jurisdiction over the affairs of the college, approving the election and voting the salaries of president and professors as late as 1786. Every wave of public opinion that affected the legislators influenced the destinies of the college. In the contests of rival factions, salaries and needed appropriations were withheld, often occasioning great inconvenience and suffering. Obnoxious opinions of the president and faculty on political subjects often involved investigation and rebuke.

The influence of English usage was shown in the original character of the corporation at Harvard. As the professors were the ruling body in the Continental schools, and the masters in the English colleges, the corporation of Harvard was composed of two classes: resident or teaching fellows, and nonresident or simply governing fellows. The former were also called fellows of the house; to them, aided by the advice of some of the ablest and most learned scholars of the country, the entire administration of the college was entrusted. They chose the president, elected their successors and associates in instruction, and were responsible for the government. In this body of seven members the title of the property was vested. The overseers were a more numerous body, and possessed the right of ratification and amendment. The occasion of this double organization will be found in the early form of colonial society. Two classes were prominent, the clergymen, the single learned class, and the civil rulers, who were alike highly honored. To these two classes, the only ones available, the oversight of our educational institutions was entrusted.

The establishment of the president and teaching fellows as a separate body for government and discipline did not take place until 1725, nearly a hundred years after the founding of the college, and as thus constituted was termed the "immediate government." Ordinary discipline had previously been in the hands of the tutors. The system of having representatives of some one of the various faculties in the corporation has continued until recent times, and has always been regarded as beneficial, as presenting the views of the teaching staff upon all questions of university policy.

The right of every tutor—for at this time there were no professors—to a seat in the corporation was early discussed, and at one time allowed by the legislature. An eventful controversy arose in 1824, upon a demand of all the instructors to representation in the governing board, who claimed that the

term "fellow" in its historic sense conferred the right to participate in the determination and decision of all university matters.
Edward Everett and Professors Ticknor and Norton advocated with great earnestness and ability the right of all members of the faculty to seats in the governing board, while the
legal members of the corporation and overseers maintained
that representation could not be claimed as a right, either from
the terms of the charter or from the history and use of the word
"fellow." This position was taken by Judges Story and Jackson, and Chief-Justice Parker and others. The decision was in
accordance with the latter view. Owing to questions of re-
organization at the time, which occasioned diverse opinions,
the application of the faculty for the election of one of their
number to the corporation was refused. Precedent dating from
the act of incorporation was in favor of such representation,
which was held desirable and legal, but not a right to be
claimed; the privilege of such election was admitted, and a
purpose to continue the former usage was expressed.

It is significant that those scholars who maintained with so
much vigor the wisdom of the choice of members of the faculty
to the governing board were familiar with foreign systems of
university administration, while the members who opposed
were lawyers, who argued strictly from the terms of the charter
and from certain legal precedents. The system of faculty representation upon the executive board is therefore not a new
one in this country.

A provision in the laws of the State of New York forbidding
a professor to hold a seat in the board of trustees was rescinded
a few years since, the repeal being favored by some of the most
accomplished scholars and educators of the state. The intimate
connection of the early state governments with questions of
religion and education was long perpetuated, even after the
original usefulness of such a relation had ceased. When the
constitution of Massachusetts of 1780 was adopted, the council and senate of the state were made members of the board of
overseers, in place of the clerical and judicial representatives
who had previously ruled. At Yale the six senior state senators

were long *ex-officio* trustees of the college. In many colleges the names of the leading state officers adorn the catalogues as honorary governors. The two parties in a legislature possibly look more leniently upon granting the charter of a new university, especially if a pecuniary grant accompanies it, when provision for such representation is inserted, as it seems to give a public character to the institution, and contesting political factions acquiesce and opposing rival claimants become silent.

It may be doubted whether any real element of strength is added to a board of trustees by the retention of these purely ornamental personages, whose names have already disappeared from the pages of many catalogues. In most cases they feel no responsibility and exercise no interest. The contribution which they make to the deliberations of the board is practically valueless. All decisions are reached without them, and they can scarcely regard their own presence save in the light of an intrusion, and naturally hesitate to be responsible for measures which a turn of the political wheel will make it impossible for them to execute. When we consider that the same state officers, by the charter of different colleges, may sustain a like relation to several institutions, the impossibility of any effective oversight becomes manifest. A public officer would especially refrain from proposing changes in the affairs of colleges which are under the exclusive control of a religious denomination.

A new element has been introduced into university administration in giving to the alumni the right of representation upon the board of overseers or trustees. It was expected that a double object would be attained by this measure; that new men, having a personal interest in the college and a recent knowledge of its needs, would become a part of the government; and that the alumni would retain a permanent connection with the institution when directly associated in its management. This may be regarded as an adaptation of the English university system, by which masters in residence for a part of the year form, at Cambridge the senate, and at Oxford the convocation,—legislative bodies to which all regulations are submitted for discussion and approval. Graduates who retain an intimate connection with the university are thus enabled to contribute the results of their learning and experience to the decision of all questions affecting the studies and government. The contrast which exists in the scholarship of English and American students upon graduation makes the experiment in the two countries far from identical. The class to which authority is entrusted in the English universities is, in extent of study and experience, far in advance of our own graduates, and is composed in most cases of professors and resident masters pursuing still further liberal studies. This difficulty is met in some colleges in this country by limiting the right to participate in these elections to graduates of five years' standing. But if it is important to continue the relation of the alumni to their university, this delay in conferring the right of suffrage till after a considerable period of separation from the college has great disadvantages. The fact that so large a portion of the alumni of our colleges is scattered throughout the land, and thus removed from an opportunity of voting in person at commencement, is obviated in some cases by a provision enabling a ballot for alumni trustees to be sent by mail, which is counted as if delivered in person. Any method which will retain the active interest of the alumni in their Alma Mater is worthy of examination and possibly of trial.

The system may now be tested by its results, as sixteen years have passed since its institution at Harvard and elsewhere. It may be premised that where there is a large and intelligent body of the alumni residing in the vicinity of a college, the attendance upon the election of trustees and an active participation in university questions are possible, and the results attained of a different order from what occurs when the alumni are widely scattered. A choice of the ablest and most influential scholars and educators may be made, whose residence will permit them to give the most careful attention to the interests of the university. But it may be questioned whether the results under the present system have equaled the expectations which had been formed. The character of those elected trustees or overseers has not greatly differed from that of those chosen previously. In most colleges a majority of the trustees have always been graduates of the colleges, and the fact of an election by the alumni did not change their essential character. Where alumni trustees have been substituted for a long list of *ex-officio* members, as at Yale, Harvard, and elsewhere, there has been a real gain. At Harvard, however, the substantial power still rests with the corporation, which is in the main a self-perpetuating body, while the overseers have only the right of confirmation of its nominations, and do not originate action. Influences affect the election of trustees by the alumni, not always favorable to securing the most efficient members. An alumnus is chosen for prominence in social or political life, or for eminence as a lawyer or clergyman, and not because he has any intelligent acquaintance with the history of education, or is qualified to judge of the demands of higher learning at the present time. Local considerations often influence the selection of candidates, and party interests are not always forgotten. Men are elected who can snatch but a hasty moment from the pressing demands of professional life, to decide upon questions affecting the permanent educational interests of the nation, and to judge of the standing and qualifications of professors in all departments of learning. Often the election is determined by a small proportion of the alumni who are able to be present, or have an interest to vote. In such cases an active local interest or an aggressive partisanship may prevail, and a choice occur based upon some remote college or society popularity. The attendance of trustees so chosen is not always secured, and only a measure of success under favorable circumstances may at present be considered as attained by the system.

The defects of these various and conflicting methods of government are obvious. Permanent and uniform principles of administration are not secured, neither is the system such that the ablest scholars become members of the governing board. All sound learning, whatever its direction, has as its chief aim the pursuit of truth. Absolute independence and freedom of investigation and instruction should be guaranteed. This liberty is impossible, save as a university is free from the strife of parties and the liability to change through the caprice of the dominant power. When a reform is necessary, a calm investigation and the study of desirable changes should be elevated above partisan considerations, and based upon scientific principles of education. The question which naturally arises is, Under what control shall our universities be placed, in order to secure that intelligent and uniform administration which shall enable them to develop in accordance with the advance of science? There can be but one answer to this, and that is that all questions relating to courses of study and the bestowal of degrees, as well as the nomination of professors, should be entrusted to the appropriate faculty for decision. It would be equally as absurd to trust the decision of an important legal question to a body of artists as to confer the control of educational questions upon a corresponding body of lawyers. Education is a science, and has a history coincident with the growth of knowledge and the development of the human mind. It is therefore in itself a historical question, as well as one of philosophy. The history of every particular science must be investigated, in order to choose wisely the methods of study in that science. It is here advocated that the faculty of a college, or of each school connected with a university, as that of law, medicine, or divinity, should be the active and responsible governing body; that it should determine the character of the instruction, and elect or nominate all professors and instructors, and should be the one unit of administration. The trustees should hold in trust the property, and confirm or reject all nominations, and in conjunction with the faculty make all the regular appropriations. It is held that the faculty is alone competent to estimate the amount and variety of instruction required, the number of departments and instructors, and the needs of the library, museums, and laboratories. It should also judge of the expediency and character of all buildings to be erected. As regards the establishment or enlargement of departments, the resident instructors, who devote all their attention to an institution of learning, are best fitted to judge of the wisdom of any change. Too often the multiplication of departments causes the regular and most essential courses of instruction to be neglected.

It may be assumed that the power to decide these questions should inhere in some one body, and we have now to consider the possible solutions of this proposition. It may rest, first, in the trustees alone, who act upon their independent judgment and knowledge of the needs of the university and the qualification of its professors. This involves a power to act without consultation with the members of the faculty, and possibly with no intelligent acquaintance with the special demands of the question at issue. But the trustees may be guided and enlightened in their opinion by the president, who is supposed to represent the views of the faculty before the trustees. Even in this case there may be an inadequate conception and representation of the wants of various departments; and without a full presentation of the views of the entire faculty, a wise consideration of all needs is impossible, a symmetrical growth will not be attained, and a single field of study may often be developed at the expense of all others. Were the faculty allowed absolute liberty of election, or were they represented by delegates who directly presented their views to the governing board, an adequate expression of all the interests involved would be obtained, and every decision or choice would be the voice of a body of scholars.

The history of every college presents numerous illustrations of action taken by the corporation directly contrary to the judgment of the faculty, and with uniformly unfavorable results. A permanent president is unknown in most foreign universities. The rector, who is chosen for a year, serves as the chairman of the senate in a German university, and a similar usage has prevailed in this country in the University of Virginia and other institutions. There is, it is true, a powerful and valuable personal element in education, but the idea of an individual shaping and reforming instruction in all departments may well provoke skepticism. The absence of fixed convictions on the part of non-educators makes them too often a mere registering board, to ratify the recommendations which are made to them. The lack of independent knowledge forces unprofessional judges to follow the formulated and positive views of one of greater experience. Thus we have either independent and unskillful action or dependence upon a single presiding authority. The latter alternative makes a body of learned men, each master of his department, the personal staff of the president. Long ago this was forseen at Harvard, and a similar proposition in the days of President Kirkland was rejected, as degrading every professor to the position of a purely ministerial officer. President Gilman, in a published paper, has well shown that it is impossible for one individual, however able, to know adequately the special needs of all departments and of the various faculties of a university. No individual is so universal that he can determine and direct the methods of instruction in the different branches of literature, science, philology, history, and philosophy. If we add to this list the requirements of special schools of advanced instruction, as law, medicine, and divinity, the impossibility of one responsible direction and supervision is readily conceded. The unity of government must be found in the various faculties. Among the many worthy and useful men who have filled the office of president of our universities, few can claim the reputation of great educators. Often—and this condition is imposed by the terms of some charters—the presidency must be held by a clergyman, and the choice may fall upon men who are not practical educators, nor familiar with the present demands and history of higher education.

The standard of instruction in all our universities must be constantly raised to keep pace with the advance of knowledge, if they are to retain their influence upon human thought and culture. To accomplish this constant development, the faculty which has a continuous existence, must be the permanent repository of power. The standing of every college depends upon the reputation and ability of the men who are there called upon to give instruction. To place the most eminent scholars where they can exercise the widest influence upon the culture of their age, and where the best resources for study and discovery are at their disposal, is an obligation which every institution owes to the cause of letters. To secure such a result, all minor considerations should be subordinated. Questions of locality, of political and personal views, should not prevail in making such choice. The judgment of those most capable of forming an estimate of the standing of scholars in various departments of learning should be obtained. Men devoted to science and letters have an acquaintance with the reputation and standing of scholars in different branches, such as an individual cannot possess. Whenever a vacancy in the academic corps occurs, the faculty should be notified to that effect, and authorized to nominate some one for that position. It is only occasionally that an election to a professorship implies that the candidate is the most capable scholar that could be chosen. Men are often appointed to positions of the highest importance who have enjoyed no special advantages for study in the field in literature, the question is not asked, What scholar is most recognized contributions to the department in which they are expected to be masters and teachers. In filling an appointment in literature, the question is not asked, What scholar is most eminent for his attainments and contributions to our knowledge of the history and development of a given language, whose opinion upon a doubtful point would have the greatest weight among scholars? An answer to such an inquiry is not impossible, and may be impartially obtained. The filling of vacancies in the Scotch universities is often deemed of so much importance that the testimonials of the different candidates are printed, in order that it may be seen upon what grounds the appointment is based. At Oxford the professor of comparative philology is appointed by the vice chancellor and the professors of Hebrew, Sanskrit, Greek, Latin, and Anglo-Saxon, men eminently qualified to judge of the standing of any candidate. The professor of English law is selected by the vice chancellor, the principal of Jesus College, the professors of

151

civil law, international law, modern history, moral philosophy, and all other professors of law. The professor of physiology is appointed with the aid of the presidents of the College of Physicians in London, of the College of Surgeons of England, and of the Royal Society; the professor of international law and diplomacy through the Lord High Chancellor, the Judge of the High Court of Admiralty, and the Secretary of State for Foreign Affairs. At both Oxford and Cambridge provisions exist for entrusting nominations to the most competent judges. A few appointments are still in the hands of Convocation, — resident masters, who are not necessarily teachers. Matthew Arnold, referring to his own election as professor of poetry, said, "Convocation made me a professor, and I am very grateful to Convocation; but Convocation is not a fit body to have the appointment of professors. Even the crown, that is the prime minister, is not the fit person to have the appointment of professors; for he is a political functionary, and feels political influence overwhelmingly. The faculty should have the right of proposing candidates to the minister." In Germany, Holland, and the schools of superior instruction in France, the members of each faculty recommend candidates to the minister of education for confirmation.

Gruber, in his sketch of the needs of the new University of Göttingen, said, in answer to the question, "How shall a large attendance of students be secured?" "The most important and the chief consideration is the employment of able, learned, and distinguished professors in all the faculties. It is of great importance, of absolute necessity, that favorable inducements should be presented to them." In discussing the qualifications of these who might be appointed, he objected to one candidate because, though clever, he was not known, and had never given instruction, and would not attract pupils. Münchhausen, the celebrated Hanoverian minister said, "If the University of Göttingen is to be distinguished above others, its professorships must be bestowed upon the most distinguished and ablest men, who will attract a great number of students." "It is the professor, and not the charter, which really makes the university," said an eminent Italian scholar. Few American colleges have acted upon this principle in the choice of professors. Men really admirable in some profession, or in some one department of knowledge, have been called to an entirely different chair. Such appointments, instead of being "a homage to intelligence and study," not only indorse superficiality and a lack of proper preparation, but do incalculable injury to a generation of students, and, in a broader sense, to the cause of learning throughout the nation. Inability on the part of a professor to impart to a student the distinct methods and training of a scientist, or a philologist, or a student of history, is to pervert and misdirect the energies, and often to vitiate the fruits of years of study. The efficiency of many a department has been permanently crippled by a mistaken appointment, and this error contains within it the seeds of wide-reaching evil consequences. No one can be elected to a position in a foreign university who has not made special contributions to the subject which he will be required to teach, and who is not known as an authority in that subject. The purpose of a university is not simply to hoard what the world knows, and to dispense elementary knowledge to immature scholars, but by investigation and study to enlarge the bounds of human knowledge. A professor should be not merely a teacher, he should be an investigator, and fitted to guide and inspire advanced study. The stream will never rise higher than its source. The neglect of these simple facts has placed men in positions of importance on the outposts of learning who, by sheer supineness, have been a hindrance to the growth of knowledge.

A college acquaintance with Latin, or Greek, or mathematics was once considered sufficient to justify an appointment to a professorship. A successful pulpit orator was held to be fitted for a professorship of rhetoric and oratory, or for that difficult position of professor of English literature. But a knowledge of literature is based upon language and history; and as no literature stands alone, a familiarity with other languages which have made contributions to it is implied, as well as an acquaintance with all the influences, religious,

153

political, and personal, which have affected literary production. Similarly, no science stands alone, and success in a single department demands proficiency in many subsidiary branches. The geologist must know chemistry and botany and zoölogy and physics, in order to make the highest contributions to knowledge in his field of study. Every branch of learning now demands a special and exclusive preparation. Ability in a single department does not prove corresponding ability in another. In the early days of American scholarship, and in the poverty of all our colleges, a professor gave instruction in the most diverse subjects. Many branches of physical science were then comparatively unknown. Language has since become a science, and the teacher's work is now an established profession, for which advanced study is requisite, either in this country or abroad.

Permanence of position is necessary to successful work on the part of the teacher. No intelligent development of any department is possible where uncertainty regarding tenure of office exists, and the highest efforts of an instructor are not obtained when he is constantly aspiring after a different position. In Germany all professorships are for life. In England most are permanent; some, however, which are more truly lectureships, are tenable for five years, with an opportunity for reëlection, as the professorship of poetry at Oxford. Many who hold such temporary positions enjoy fellowships, benefices, and other university appointments at the same time. A position with a limited duration can never command the highest scholarship and ability. A scholar, in selecting his field of work, cannot view with equanimity the necessity of early removal. Frequent changes in the teaching force of a university mean a varying and doubtful standard of instruction, new methods, untried men, and uncertain results. A university cannot exist with an unorganized faculty, forever tentative in its men and measures, — an attitude which cannot but be regarded as a humiliating confession of weakness.

For subordinate positions in a university, service for a fixed period is advantageous, if it holds out a reasonable prospect of promotion in case success is achieved. When this fact is established, a limited tenure loses all advantage, and becomes injurious, as offering no permanent inducement, and creating unrest in the instructor. The report of the Schools Inquiry Commission in England presents a variety of opinions upon this question in its application to the educational institutions of the kingdom. The principles of civil service reform should prevail in university administration. No position should be regarded as the private property of an individual. Graded promotion should be introduced, as perpetual subordination paralyzes all ambition and growth.

In comparing the French and German systems of appointment, it is manifest that in perfection of detail, which makes the whole educational system of the country a delicately constructed machine, France presents a more compact educational organization than Germany. To be an *agrégé,* that is to have a diploma authorizing a candidate to hold the office of professor in a *lycée* or *faculté,* the utmost security is required. An examination covering the entire range of instruction which the candidate will have to give has first to be passed. Five years' preliminary experience in teaching is necessary. Records of service and seniority are strictly kept. To be a *professeur titulaire,* the candidate must be a doctor or member of the Institute.

The strength of the German university consists largely in the *Privatdocenten,* from whom the professorships are filled. This class of authorized independent instructors, attached to a university, is engaged in vindicating its right to a higher position by study and instruction. These subordinate teachers often make contributions recognized as of great value, and attain a world-wide reputation in their various departments before promotion. Only in a university after the German model, where *Lehrfreiheit* and *Lernfreiheit* are found, could this important class exist. Here, where there is a fixed curriculum, with all its parts adequately provided for, there is scarcely room for an additional class of instructors, without great modifications in our present system. Academic jealousy would perhaps regard their claims and their rivalry as an infringement upon established rights. Nothing of the kind exists abroad; there is the most generous and helpful relation existing between the Privatdocenten and the professor, and the instruction of the former is carefully provided for in the schedule of lectures of each semester. It is a defect in the French system that it fails to present the opportunity of free study and instruction which develops the highest gifts of those who are to become public teachers. The German system has this advantage over that of English fellows: the Privatdocenten not only investigate, but teach as well. Study apart from teaching often becomes unpractical and theoretical, while teaching without investigation becomes narrow and technical. The presence of such a class of young scholars, full of vital energy, acts as a powerful impulse to keep fresh the quality of instruction given by the professors.

The verdict of publication, which is always insisted upon in Germany preliminary to an appointment to a professor's chair, is valuable as a test of capacity for investigation. A system which assumes nothing for granted in the choice of professors, but always demands some production as a test of merit, would elevate the character and work of all candidates for positions. We could then dispense with paper testimonials, and the personal element in making appointments would be largely eliminated. Elections to positions in our higher institutions of learning should be so conducted that a choice would become the goal of a worthy ambition.

That a reform is possible in the position which professors hold in a university cannot be doubted. The present method of appointment has not secured the ablest men, and the external government is not such as to accomplish the best results. It is useless to utter the truism that American universities are not on a par with European; the fact is too painfully manifest, and a continuance of the present system is powerless to effect what is needed. It does not secure the best men; it does not place the best scholars in a position where their views can exercise the widest influence; but under the jurisdiction of a loosely constituted board, chosen often for the most diverse reasons. The universities owe a higher debt to national education than they have ever paid; they have not accomplished for national learning that which might reasonably be expected of them.

A source of weakness in the past has been the strictness with which appointments in minor colleges have been limited to their own graduates. To fill certain chairs, a laborious search is often made for one of the alumni of the college who, by chance, may possess some part of the qualifications needed. Nothing of this kind exists abroad. It is not asked where the scholar received his degree, if his merits point him out as the most desirable candidate. Men are constantly called from one university to another. Eminence in any branch of scholarship finds instant recognition, and that without envy.

Independence of the changes wrought by the success of a new party in power, or a new shade of popular opinion, is essential to a permanent and intelligent university administration.

The relations between the faculty and the governing board have been already indicated. In order that the voice of the faculty may be heard in all questions affecting the welfare of the university, and to prevent them, while sitting apparently in the places of authority, from being powerless to correct abuses and carry out needed reforms, it is necessary that representatives of the faculty should become members of the corporation. Without any change in any university charter, it is within the power of the corporation to take independently such action as will effect this result. The faculty should be authorized to elect annually two or more delegates to sit with the corporation, participating in its deliberations, and expressing freely their views on all questions; becoming thus the medium of communication between the faculty and trustees. Changes in the charter should embody the right of resident instructors to representation. That provision in the statutes of several states which forbids professors in a college from becoming members of the corporation is so framed as to exclude those who have devoted a life-time to the study of educational questions from having any voice in settling the most important interests connected with academic culture. It has been shown how all European examples are contrary to the American system, and that our early colleges found the principle here advocated useful in its operations. Members of the faculty of Harvard have served in the corporation and in the board of overseers repeatedly during the present century, as in the case of Henry Ware, who was an overseer from 1820 to 1830, of Dr. James Walker, who was a fellow, both of whom were academic professors; James Freeman Clarke was an overseer from 1866 to 1872, and Judge Story was a fellow nearly the entire period in which he held his professorship in the law school. The wisdom with which the finances of Harvard were managed by the corporation of seven members, of whom a portion were resident instructors, shows the practicability of the plan here urged; and the disorder which followed a transfer, the lavish outlay and subsequent retrenchment, show how necessary is a competent acquaintance with the needs of all departments for judicious expenditure. The principle of autonomy in the faculty which is here advocated prevails in most professional schools in this country, in its leading scientific school, and in the admirable Museum of Comparative Zoölogy in Cambridge: having been thus successfully tested, its application may safely be extended to the academic faculties.

The bestowal of degrees should also rest with the faculty. It is quite anomalous that a body of non-educators should confer all marks of honor in letters, where they are necessarily dependent upon the judgment of those who give instruction. Those institutions which continue to bestow honorary degrees usually do so without any consultation with the appropriate faculty. Lawyers who have attained a local success, popular clergymen and patrons whose benefactions enrich the university treasury, commencement orators and congressmen, are the recipients of these valuable badges. Upon what basis of of scholarship these degrees are conferred no one has ever attempted to ascertain. The University of Virginia, the Cornell University, and the Johns Hopkins University are, I believe, the only prominent institutions which have never bestowed these honors except for the completion of a regular course of advanced study. No satisfactory reason has ever been given why the immediate control of a university should be taken from the faculty, a body of competent scholars, and entrusted to others with less experience in educational questions. The president was originally a teacher, *primus inter pares*, like the rector of a German university, — a relation which has been changed by the unwise limitation of the powers of the faculty, and by the increasing needs of a general executive officer. A feeling of responsibility upon the part of each professor for all measures is necessary to give dignity to his work. A sense that his private interests are intimately associated with the success of the institution with which he is connected imparts increased efficiency, gives conscientiousness and fidelity in the discharge of duty, and a watchful care of all its interests.

The size of the faculty and its complex character make it advisable in many universities to elect a limited number from various departments to form a senate or council, to whom a general oversight of the administration and discipline may be entrusted. The senate should receive the instructions of the general faculty from time to time, and as an executive committee discuss and prepare measures to be laid before the greater faculty, and receive all applications for advanced degrees. There is a great waste of time in the cumbersome deliberations of a large body, which might be saved by entrusting minor matters to a standing committee, acting under general rules. Within the faculty an organization of the various related departments is valuable.

Few universities have a constitution fixing the mutual relations of the faculties and trustees, of the various departments, of professors and subordinates, their rights and times of service. These important matters are undetermined, and hence usage is variable and inconsistent, and disastrous consequences ensue.

159

A question which affects the general public, as well as concerns all our institutions for secondary education, is the character and value of the degrees which are conferred by different institutions. It must be confessed that a higher moral sentiment should be aroused in the various colleges of our country, to protect the people against diplomas issued by colleges and scientific and professional schools for superficial merit. The poverty of many schools, and their dependence upon numbers for their support, contributes to produce this unsatisfactory state of affairs. The modern haste in entering a profession, and the unwillingness to submit to thorough and long-continued study, have aided to bring about the present situation. An acquaintance with a few law books and a few facts regarding procedure is enough to make a lawyer, and many a physician receives his degree with little knowledge of chemistry, botany, physics, or comparative anatomy. Two solutions are possible: first, by state superintendence of our educational institutions, regulating the requirements for both academic and professional degrees. When it is considered that the school system of Germany in its present form is the product of the present century, that its excellence largely dates from the time when William von Humboldt occupied the office of Minister of Public Instruction in Prussia, we cannot doubt that a similar success is possible in America. The state, by appointing a board of examiners, consisting of the ablest representative scholars from different colleges, could prescribe a course by which a degree might be conferred under the seal of the state, which would certify to scholarship in the liberal arts and sciences, or confer the title of civil engineer or the right to practice law or medicine within its limits. Such a provision would cause courses of study in law and medicine in all schools to be assimilated to the requirements of a state examination. Assuredly, the state has sufficient interest in the orderly administration of justice and in the lives and health of its citizens to take measures to secure such valuable results.

The action of a single state would harmonize the conflicting standards of the many colleges within its borders. A national conference, like those held in Jena in 1848 and in Berlin in 1849, which at that time, unfortunately, failed to accomplish what was hoped, but were a valuable contribution to the discussion of educational questions, might lead the way to a higher standard of study and examinations throughout the country.

A second solution may be found in the voluntary union of the faculties of the different colleges of a section or a state, like the conferences held annually by delegates from the New England colleges, which have aided to elevate and make uniform the requirements for admission. A commission which agreed upon some equal or parallel conditions for the bestowal of different degrees might not secure uniformity, but would set up a goal towards which educational efforts would be directed.

The proposition which is here advocated, namely, the participation of the faculty in the government, has been shown to be the prevailing system in the Continental universities, to have been in part the usage at Harvard for one hundred and fifty years, and to be, with shades of difference, the practice in the English universities. In one or two of the great universities of this country, and in its most successful scientific school, the government rests practically with the faculty. The sense of responsibility which is felt for the prosperity of a university on the part of all the professors is one of the most valuable results of this system. Instead of being merely assigned to a department of instruction, and administering laws laid down for them, powerless to remedy flagrant abuses and errors of government, they become the active custodians of the order and the culture of the university. The German and English universities are the centre of the learning of those countries; they are the seat of an enthusiastic and chivalrous scholarship. The organization which has made these universities so remarkable in literary industry and productions is certainly worthy of consideration, if investigation and critical scholarship are to find a home in this country. If this nation is to bear an equal part in the advance of learning, we certainly cannot rest content with the methods and instrumentalities of the past. Old organizations must be expanded and assume a new life; the connection of instruction with investigation, which has been ignored so long in England, must be recognized. Study without a practical aim becomes dreamy and unproductive, while entire absorption in the work of instruction renders advanced study impossible. A lack of unity of action on the part of our higher institutions of learning has given rise to the varying standard of instruction, and to the unequal value of degrees; even where a fixed curriculum of study exists, designed to secure the general culture of students, greater uniformity of action is possible and desirable.

Another aim, akin to that which has been suggested, would be a unifying of the number and meaning of the different degrees. State control of education abroad establishes a certain uniformity in the value of degrees. It would be easy to mention a score or more of first degrees which are conferred in different colleges of our country. Many are practically meaningless; others are worse than useless. Each college gives to the degree of bachelor of literature, of science, and philosophy whatever signification it chooses, and the public acquiesces with a quiet skepticism, and an increased conviction that under the present system all degrees are worthless. The reckless creation of new degrees thus produces merited fruit, but a result in which the cause of education suffers.

Among the subjects, then, which demand consideration in higher education are the constitution of the governing board in a university, the relation of the faculty to the general administration, the organization of faculties and departments, and the question of academic degrees.

9

Shall Women Go to College?

E. R. Sill

The "previous question," fundamental to the whole subject of the education of women, so central that the least divergence there will emerge as a large difference of view as to the usefulness of giving women a liberal education at all, is the question—to state it baldly and flatly—*What is woman for?* Has she, that is to say, an independent significance in the universe, such as man is assumed to have; or has she only a subordinate and merely accessory relation to him? It is useless to expect any agreement on the more superficial question of women's education between persons who hold the two opposite views of this underlying question. These two opposite views are:

1. That woman is for herself and for the community; for man, no doubt, but only in the same sense that man is for her. This view implies that the natural relations between the sexes in civilized society are relations of equality. However much they may be relations of difference and division of labor, the difference does not depend on any natural distinction in grade of intelligence, nor the division of labor involve any distinction in grade of education. It implies, in short, that one sex has just as much individual significance in the universe as the other. This may be called the modern view. It is, however, even in

Reprinted from *Century Magazine*, Vol. 32, No. 2, June 1886, pp. 323-326.

modern times, only the view of the most enlightened nations; and in those nations a view chiefly confined to the best-educated communities; and in those communities not apt to be the view of persons wholly unaccustomed to the society of superior women. For this is emphatically one of those subjects on which the old adage is true, that "seeing is believing."

2. That woman is for man, as subordinate and accessory. This may be called the mediaeval, Asiatic, or Miltonic view. It implies that the unit and center of this world is man. The air was created for him to breathe, the herb of the field to furnish him sustenance, the beast thereof to do his bidding; and among these conveniences a bountiful Providence added woman. There have been many varieties of this general view, from that which admits that woman has a soul, and regards her as man's vizier, or housekeeper, or adviser in chief, down to that which regards her as his mere slave and drudge. Practically, all these varieties of the Miltonic view have a tendency to reduce themselves to the last. Theoretically, however, they usually take the form of regarding her in the conveniently ambiguous light of a "helpmate"—actual wife-beating not being popular, at least in this country, among the native population.

Even on this theory of the subordinate "helpmate," it would seem worth while so to educate a woman that she should be a "mate," and capable of "helping," in the higher activities of thought as well as in the lower ones of frivolity or drudgery. But the more radical question is, why should the man be assumed to be the unit, and the woman his "helpmate," any more than the reverse arrangement? Those who quote the Old Testament to support this view should remember that the same authority has been quoted, as every one knows, to sustain human slavery in its more obvious form; yet we have taken the liberty of extirpating that from modern civilization. Is it not time to admit in plain terms, since we have already admitted it in so many institutions of society, that the one sex has equal significance in the world with the other? To suppose that one sex is the integer, and the other a mere cipher having no value except as appended to it, is simply one final relic of barbarism. The unit of civilized society is not the man, or the woman,—it is the family. It is no more the chief end of woman to glorify man and serve him forever, than it is man's chief end to sustain that relation to her. It is her privilege, doubtless, to be the mother of his children; but is it not equally his privilege to be the father of hers? The higher any community rises in the scale of civilization, the more do men and women become equal "mates," equally "helpers," in the family and community life.

To both sexes, then, and to both sexes alike, the important thing in youth is that the mind should be helped to attain to its best possibilities. It belongs not to man's rights nor to woman's rights, but to human rights. The birthright of each — whatever the obstacles to laying hold of it — is a complete intelligence. And certainly the burden of proof lies with any one who asserts that the course of liberal culture productive of educated men would fail to produce educated women. Vague reference to some mysterious "difference" between the male and the female mind is of no value in supporting such an assertion.

It needs to be shown in what precise region of the mental faculties any given branch of liberal study would fail to form and inform a woman's mind as it does a man's. It would be interesting to know, for example, just what corner of the intellect would be affected differently in the two sexes by, say, algebra, or English history, or the science of astronomy.

To insist on definite statements in this way from the opponent of a liberal education for women, would be to discover in many cases that the wish is father to the thought. He is compelled to admit, at last, that he has no desire to see women completely rational. If he does not quite say frankly, as an intelligent foreigner once said to the writer, "Sometimes it is not good that a woman should know too much; it makes trouble in the family!" yet he evidently is apprehensive of some indefinable danger from the tendency of modern ideas on this subject. His fancy seems to cling to the primitive ideal of the silly and adorable thing, whose confessed inferiority mingles an element of self-complacency in his devotion.

What the exact ideal of a woman is, in the minds of those who express such fears, we do not see distinctly stated. It is doubtful if they would like to state it in plain English, even in the bosom of their families; perhaps there least of all. But this ideal may be inferred from the character of the education to which they seem to look for its production. This mild form of education, favored by those who fear the effect on the feminine mind of the too robust college course, calls for courses of study somewhat tenderer and prettier, and especially somewhat easier. They are apparently expected to produce a fair being equipped about as follows. Her disposition should be soft and pillowy. Her will, or any rudiment of it that may have begun to show itself, should have been gently caused to disappear. Of the intellectual powers, perception would probably have been cultivated to whatever limited extent it is absolutely required in good society, but not to a degree that would force on her attention any facts unsuited to her sphere. The judgment would have been delicately stimulated, but not to any revolting extent. The memory would be expected to be well developed, as being convenient in housekeeping, but coupled with a certain felicity of forgetting any little matters that would not conduce to domestic peace. In the region of the feelings, the regulation of this special feminine education would be truly difficult. For while sensibility in general would be the strong point in the highly specialized femininity, there are obviously certain feelings which she should not be permitted to have, even though surgery in the cerebral lobes were required for their extirpation, — the desire of knowledge, for example, or the aspiration after intellectual enlargement, or the sense of justice, or the desire of power. But the sweet sensibilities should be hers; the hunger for approbation and applause; the capacity for gazing upon sublime objects, notably upon the males of her household, with wonder, love, and awe.

Happily this is not the only extant ideal of what a woman should be. There is another ideal; one that has perhaps existed from the beginning of civilized history; one that certainly now exists in an increasing number of minds. It is the ideal of a woman having all the mental endowment that the most fully equipped man has ever had; and having this "capability of godlike reason," not latent, but trained by the most thoroughgoing education to complete activity. It has made it the easier

for the world to retain this ideal that all along, in spite of prodigious hindrances, it has persisted in revealing itself as an
accomplished fact.

For those, then, who are disposed to believe that not one sex
merely, but the human mind in general, is intended to be intelligent, the question arises, Is a college education, in the
case of women as of men, the best available means to that
end?

Underlying this inquiry, also, there is a "previous question"
which needs to be asked and answered before we can see
just where we stand on this matter of the college training. It is
the question, *What is a college for?* This question is seldom
raised, because the discovery is not often made that we differ
upon it. But if we will take the trouble to look closely, we shall
find that precisely upon this point there is the greatest diversity
of opinion.

Many seem to suppose that the purpose of a college is to
fit a man—being as he is—for some special pursuit. Its true
purpose, on the contrary, is to take the crude material of a man
and make of him far more than he is, or ever would have been
without some such liberal culture. It aims to determine, not
what the man shall get in this or that pursuit, but what he shall
be, whatever his pursuit. It proposes not merely that the man
shall get a living, but that he shall get a life. The notion that
the purpose of a college is to fit a man to get the greatest
amount of money or reputation in the least amount of time in
some particular occupation, belongs with that whole Philistine
view which regards existence as only a vulgar "struggle" after
political preferment or other squalid prize, and which looks
upon education therefore, as but a sort of Fagin's training
for this "struggle of life"; whereas, in fact, if a liberal culture
has any one end more marked than another, it is to lift a man
above the desire or the necessity for any such feverish and selfish "struggle." It sets before him higher aims. It makes it
seem shameful and contemptible to "struggle" for the office
or the reputation which should seek the man, not be "strug-
gled" for by him. It equips him with powers that make the
getting of an honorable living, or of respectable position and

influence in the community, too easy a matter to seem very exciting as the prize of a life-long "struggle." If the purpose of a college were to fit a man for some one of three or four special pursuits, there might be an argument against the admission of women to college, in the assumption that these pursuits are unsuited to women. But the colleges would never have been any such power in the world as they have been and are, had they been built on that narrow basis. Their purpose is to give a man, as a preliminary to any or all occupations, that complete intelligence, that breadth of power and inner resourse, which no special training ever could furnish; which, in fact, both a narrow special training and the special pursuit afterward, in our system of extreme division of labor, must (to the apparent present gain of society, no doubt, but to the loss of the individual) oppose and curtail. All the more need that, to the begin with, the man should be broadly educated, no matter what bread-occupation shall claim and confine him afterward. The college courses have grown out of the instinctive hunger for this complete intelligence. They consist, therefore, not of occupative, but of educative studies. These studies have been chosen—and still are retained, notwithstanding the complaints of persons who seem impervious to this point—not so much with reference to their being convenient to the man hereafter in one or another pursuit, as with reference to their being necessary to him now, while still capable of organic mental growth, in that nearly miraculous change from a raw youth to an educated man. If, for example, the *literae humaniores* are still retained in college courses, it is from a settled conviction, based upon both theory and experiment, that these studies are best fitted to "educe the man."

There can be, then, but one rational answer to our second question. The purpose of a college is to produce, first of all, a completely intelligent mind. It is a preparation, not for this or that special profession, but for the great common profession of living the intellecutal life, no matter by what particular occupation this is to be maintained.

What is there, now, in woman's nature or woman's natural pursuits that should debar her from the privilege of such mental development? Is reasonableness a different thing in the two sexes? Is intelligence a word of two genders? When we have once come out of the Asiatic view of the natural insignificance of half the human race, it is a little hard to see why the son should be instructed and the daughter left ignorant; why the husband should be a philosopher and the wife a fool. If a one-sided and cruel custom as to this matter has come down to us with all the absurd sacredness of a long ancestry, it is time now to do away with it. A woman should claim from life a completely developed intelligence, and life should claim it from a woman, no less than in the case of a man. She needs it as a wife no less than he as a husband. They need it equally as parents. It belongs to them alike, as members of the community, as makers of public opinion, as readers, thinkers, and writers, as partners in the common business of living.

And if it be agreed that it is as undesirable for one six to be left ignorant and feeble-witted as for the other, and that the college course is, to say the least, one good way to prevent this, the remaining question is, *Shall the two sexes get this college training together?*

It certainly would seem natural and reasonable—unless some very serious objection to it is discovered—that the two sexes, growing up together in the family, studying together in school, associated together all the rest of their lives in the work and play of society, should also receive their liberal culture together. It would seem an obviously unwholesome contrivance that should, for this single period of four years out of a lifetime, compel an artificial separation into two flocks: a scholastic monastery on the one hand, a scholastic nunnery on the other. As if history had not plainly enough declared the results of such unnatural contrivances! And the question forces itself on the mind, Is not this whole superstition of a separate sex education a relic of the dark ages? Is it not a part of the mediaeval plan of shutting women up in towers; a modified form of the Mohammedan custom of forcing them to muffle up their heads, or peer out upon the world with one eye?

Our conservative friends who still hold to some modified

form of this mediaeval and Asiatic view of "woman's sphere," have been able to retard the progress toward a full education for women, at complete or co-education colleges, by several ingenious objections.* One such objection, quite plausible some years ago, before the experiment had been thoroughly tried, was the fear that the health of young women would suffer by attending a complete college. It is too late to make this pretext prosper now. Experience has shown that a college is a peculiarly healthy place for young women. The fear that the use of the brain would endanger the health belonged with the old notion that an ignorant person has a better chance for life than an educated one. It was a notion that easily arose in simple minds. The brutes were seen to be healthy; "argal," the nearer a man could keep to the level of the brutes the better.

Those who have sustained the prodigious toils of the college course in comparative safety, will not be likely to take these perils of brain-activity too seriously. They will be disposed to agree with the doctrine of the physiologists, that the brain, like other organs, is meant to be used. Not only is its use not detrimental to health, but it is conducive to health. It should not be overworked, neither should the muscles; but it should not be left torpid any more than the lungs or the liver. Thought is as natural and wholesome an activity as breathing is. And if for the one sex, it is difficult to see why not for the other.

At all events, the stubborn fact remains that the young women in complete colleges, where the two sexes pursue together a course of liberal study, enjoy excellent health. They are good eaters, good walkers, free from morbid states of either mind or body, cheerful, animated, industrious. Why

* Let us do justice to the usefulness of a conservative opposition during any reform. It would have been a misfortune if co-education had suddenly become the fashion, so as to drift a multitude of frivolous young women, without earnest aims of solid preparation, into the colleges. It was well for college faculties to learn gradually, by a few isolated instances, the impossibility of harboring any such class of persons.

should they not be, with their "plain living and high thinking," their regular habits, their freedom from the alternate excitement and *ennui* of society life? The daily contact with high-minded teachers; the dignified plane of occupations; the natural, open-air relations with fellow-students; the busy intellectual interests of the place, — these are all guarantees of physical as well as spiritual health. It is certainly a life that contrasts favorably, in both these respects, with either the feverish emptiness of the fashionable world, the dull home-life of "quiet families," where ideas do not greatly penetrate, or the bovine existence of the illiterate country girl.

One element of culture, at least, can never be gained elsewhere so well, either by man or woman, as in a great college of both sexes; an "element" of culture that might better be called its very soul. It is the breaking-up of provincialism; the learning of the existence of the other point of view; the perception of the common human egotisms and limitations, and so the inference of one's own. And one final provincialism of the mind there is, which a unisexual college certainly never would have any power to eradicate; it would rather have an influence to strengthen its growth. It is the provincialism of the exclusively sex point of view itself. It is the tendency, that is to say, characteristic of the crude and brute condition of both men and women, to see in the opposite sex only an opposite sex.

No one has any business with this subject who fails to appreciate its gravity. It is not a question to be treated flippantly or dogmatically. The whole matter is still in the stage of experiment, and it is one of those experiments that need careful handling. But we are already in a position to see that many supposed risks attending co-education were fanciful, not real. Its difficulties and dangers may almost be said to resolve themselves into a single one — a great one, but it may be and has been met. It is the danger that, through some easy shifting of responsibility, or some happy-go-lucky good-nature, the college will suffer itself to be a mere play-ground for idle and frivolous young men and women.

If it is to attempt to be a complete college — that is to say, a complete family — it must throw to the winds the sentimental idea that anybody, no matter what his or her morals, manners, pursuits, or purposes, must be permitted to dangle about the institution indefinitely. Its governing body must stand *in loco parentis,* at least to extent of excluding flirts and other fools, of whatever age or sex, both from the students and (let us dare to say) from the faculty. And be it always remembered that, in this matter of co-education at least, no college can hope to succeed with a cartilaginous backbone in its highest official position.

We have alluded to one embarrassment in discussing this question of co-education. It is, namely, the disposition in the opponents of the modern idea to escape the frank expression of their fundamental objection to it. Other reasons are put forward by them, such as anxieties concerning health, morals, etc. — anxieties wholly unsupported by the results of actual experiment — when the real point often is that they do not heartily approve of the thorough education of women anywhere, or by any plan. So that it would always be as well, before wasting breath in a discussion of ways and means, to get a categorical answer to the blunt inquiry, "Do you believe in women's knowing as much as men, anyway?"

But there is a second embarrassment. It lies in the fact that the most influential opposition to co-education, after all, is not open to any reasoning whatever on the subject. For it is an open secret, to those who are familiar with the really dominant forces in our great educational establishments, that the power behind the throne is not altogether an intellectual, but partly a social power. It consists, namely, in the instincts, the prejudices, the convictions — if we choose to dignify them by that term — of those estimable leaders of the best academic society, who are accustomed to a social supremacy based on quite other sorts of prestige, and who naturally shrink from the inauguration of a new régime. This conservative social power is armed with many gentle ferocities for both male and female reformers, and will be apt to yield but very slowly to the march of events and ideas.

What the condition of human affairs will be when they shall have, not as an exception in a privileged class, but as a rule in all classes, the advantage of two completely intelligent and rational sexes, instead of one, it is impossible accurately to know; but that the world will then enjoy a more symmetrical and steady progress, it seems safe to predict.

10

The Education of Freedmen

Harriet Beecher Stowe

It now remains to give a brief survey of the permanent institutions which have grown up out of this educational enthusiasm which has united all Christian churches since the
war.

The American Missionary Society, formed in 1846, as an
anti-slavery missionary body, stood ready equipped to go into
the field and aid and supplement the course of Northern
benevolence. All denominations availed themselves of its
patronage, which was entirely unsectarian. As the work
broadened and increased, however, each denomination had its
own separate society, carried on in its own special way.

The American Missionary Society has planted one college
or university for the colored people in each of the Southern
States.

These are Hampton Institute, Virginia; Berea College,
Kentucky; Fiske University, Nashville, Tennessee; Atlanta
University, Atlanta, Georgia; Talladega College, Talladega,
Alabama; Tongaloo University, Tongaloo, Mississippi;
Straight University, New Orleans, Louisiana. The society
has also seventeen institutions of a lower grade scattered
through the different Southern States, and eight common

Reprinted from *North American Review*, Vol. 129, No. 272, July
1879, pp. 81-94.

schools. It is calculated that 60,000 freedmen are annually instructed in these institutions.

In 1865 the Presbyterian Church began its separate and distinctive work for the colored race, organizing a Presbyterian Committee of Missions for Freedmen. From 1865 to 1870 the receipts of this Committee averaged $27,000 per year.

The Presbyterian Church sought to cultivate intelligence among freedmen by planting and maintaining among them church and school conjointly. This specialty of parochial schools characterized the movement both of the Presbyterians and the Episcopalians. Besides their parochial schools the Presbyterian Church maintains five endowed institutions, namely: Biddle Memorial Institute, Charlotte, North Carolina, with three professors, three assistant professors, 124 pupils —value of property, $17,000; Scotia Seminary for Colored Girls, Concord, North Carolina, 105 pupils—value of property, $2,500; Wallingford Academy, Charleston, South Carolina, one professor, 261 pupils—value of property, $13,450; Mainerd School, Chester, South Carolina, one professor, 231 pupils—value of property, $3,600; Fairfield Normal School, Winnsborough, South Carolina, one professor, 184 pupils— value of property, $3,500: total, six professors, three assistant professors, 905 pupils—value of property, $40,050.

The Baptist Church has not been behindhand in zeal for this work. It has invested in it $716,273, and has under its charge, besides its churches and parochial schools, the following endowed institutions: Wayland Seminary, Washington, District of Columbia, with one professor, 92 pupils; Richmond Institute, Richmond, Virginia, one professor, 74 pupils; Shaw University, Raleigh, North Carolina, one professor, 230 pupils; Benedict Institute, Columbia, South Carolina, one professor, 118 pupils; Augusta Institute, Augusta, Georgia, one professor, 52 pupils; Nashville Institute, Nashville, Tennessee, one professor, 136 pupils; Leland University, New Orleans, Louisiana, one professor, 92 pupils; total, 795.

The Methodist Episcopal Church, fitted by her peculiar

organization and system of itinerant preaching for efficient action in this field, also went into it with zeal according to knowledge.

The following permanently endowed educational institutions attest her success: Central Tennessee College, Nashville, Tennessee; Shaw University, Holly Springs, Mississippi; Claflin University and Baker Institute, Orangeburg, South Carolina; Clarke University and Theological Seminary, Atlanta, Georgia; New Orleans University and Thomson Biblical Institute, New Orleans, Louisiana; Wiley University, Marshall, Texas; Haven Normal School, Waynesborough, Georgia; Rust Biblical and Normal Institute, Huntsville, Alabama; La Tèche Seminary, Baldwin, Louisiana; Bennett Seminary, Greensborough, North Carolina; Richmond Normal School, Richmond, Virgina; Cookman Institute, Jacksonville, Florida; Centenary Biblical Institute, Baltimore, Maryland; Orphans' Home, Baldwin, Louisiana.

The Episcopal Church also has entered this field of Christian labor with zeal and success.

In the late Missionary Conference of the Episcopal Church in New York, the Right Reverend Bishop Dudley, of Kentucky, addressed the Conference upon this subject, and commenced by saying that the Episcopal Church was more to blame for the ignorance of the Southern negroes than any other body, because the members of that Church had been the largest owners of them in slavery. He added: "We are here to consider what we shall do, by the providence of God, now that the relation of the races has been changed; and remember that I as a Southern man am ready to thank God for this result of the civil war, and I am not here in any other sense than that we are come to consult how best to carry the gospel of Jesus Christ, as this Church has received it, to those four millions of people, who stand to-day in that land from which I come as free men, as citizens, yes, as a mighty power in the body politic, who are going to control, maybe, the legislation of this land. I remember once to have heard that apostolic man who

177

has just taken his seat say to the men of New York what I want to say to the men of America to-day about this race. The Bishop of Minnesota said to the men of New York, 'You have got to take care of the poor people of this land or they will take care of you'; and so I say, 'You have got to take care of these people whom God hath set free from their bondage, and to whom have been given such civil rights that now the vote of one of them is just as mighty a factor in the land where I live as mine, or that of the Governor of the State—we have got to take care of them, or they are going to take care of us.' "

The report of the Episcopal Commission of Home Missions to colored people gives a list of thirty-seven missionary stations among these people, each supporting a missionary, a church, a parochial school, and a Sunday-school.

The system of the Episcopal Church seems in many respects exactly adapted to bring into an orderly and edifying use some of the peculiarities of the colored race. Her ritual, admitting responses, chanting processionals, and some scenic and aesthetic effect, will be attractive; while her liturgy, with its constant reiteration of Scripture reading, its collects, its affecting sacramental forms, will be a constant source of religious instruction. An effort being made in this Church to prepare an educated colored ministry is also specially interesting, as showing the decrease of the unchristian prejudice against color in a denomination which contains a great body of the former slaveholders. Rev. A. T. Twing, in his report to the Domestic Committee, September 1, 1878, gives this instance: "In a diocese at the capital of the State, where the beginning was with a few children taught under great opposition from the whole community by a noble presbyter and his wife, the result is—he being dead, but yet speaking—a Sunday-school of three or four hundred, instructed and sustained by the best people of the parish, the former and bitter prejudice having passed away. The present rector, honoring the memory and course of his predecessor, looks forward, not to a mission-chapel in an obscure and out-of-the-way place, but to an enlargement of the church to proportions ample for the accommodation of colored as well as white worshipers, and to the day not far distant when he hopes to have with the hearty approval of his people an antiphonal choir of white choristers on one side and black choristers on the other, and when a colored clergyman will minister with him at God's holy alter." This will certainly be a consummation worthy a Catholic and Apostolic Church.

To this summary of the various educational institutions of different Christian bodies must be added a notice of Howard University in the national capital.

This institution, organized primarily under the national patronage by the Freedman's Bureau, offers equal advantages of education to all, without distinction of creed, race, or sex.

The departments of instruction at Howard University are as follows:

1. The Academic Department, including five courses of study, viz.: *a,* the *Model School Course* of three years in the elementary English branches (students completing this course are prepared to begin either of the three following); *b,* the *Normal Course* of three years, adapted to those who have the work of teaching in view; *c,* the *Literary Course* of four years, designed to furnish a good practical education for those who are unable to take the full college curriculum; *d,* the *Classical Preparatory Course* of three years; and *e,* the *Classical College Course* of four years.

2. The Medical Department.

3. The Law Department.

4. The Theological Department.

The institution has a library of seven thousand volumes of general literature, and each professional department has its library. There are a cabinet of minerals containing four thousand specimens and a museum of history.

In the medical department, such are the advantages that a majority of the students are white. The theological department has about thirty students—some quite mature in age—in various preparatory, special, and regular courses, some of whom are already preachers, in a humble way, in their respective denominations. In the other departments worthy young persons are seeking to prepare for all the different vocations in life. They come from the abodes of poverty, and help themselves so far as opportunity offers, by labor, at leisure hours, and during vacations. But such earnings are usually insufficient. The charge for tuition is only twelve dollars a year, and room-rent is the same, while board is furnished at about ten dollars per month. No charge is made for tuition or room-rent to students for the gospel ministry.

With extensive buildings and grounds, the institution has no available endowments. Formerly it had liberal aid from the Freedman's Bureau, which no longer operates. Its temporary dependence is on rents, tuition, fees, and other scanty resources. With endowments for the professorships it could not only permanently sustain the present limited arrangements for instruction, but could greatly enlarge them to the advantage of the interests concerned. If permanent scholarships of $1,000 or $1,500 each could be secured, the best talent among the needy might be educated for important service. Even with temporary annual scholarships of fifty or a hundred dollars, the number of deserving students could soon be doubled. Often a donation of fifteen or twenty dollars will suffice to supplement the resources of a student so as to enable him to go through the year. A large addition to the female students could be made if friends would enable the institution to render slight aid. Churches, Sunday-schools, and individuals will here find a noble opportunity to do good, by contributions of money, clothing, bedding, stationery.

The entire floating debt of over $100,000 has been paid off within three years, and the only incumbrance on the buildings is $11,000. There is every reason to hope that this noble institution may receive that aid of which it is worthy. We have not space in this article to particularize the different institutions which in each State are working in this field of education. The writer has been through an extensive examination of the latest catalogues of each one up to the present year. Certain points are observable in which they all agree:

1. The use either of tobacco or of ardent spirits in any form is prohibited to pupils.

2. While all of them allow of the co-education of the sexes, such judicious regulations exist, with regard to all the proprieties and decorums of life, that no breath of suspicion or scandal has arisen in this regard. The presence of the two sexes is so guarded as to produce the delicacy, refinement, and purity of a Christian family.

3. All of them are guided by an earnest religious influence, and make it their object to enlighten the quick religious sensibility of the colored race, and bring it under the control of intelligent faith.

Berea College, in Kentucky, has accomplished the great point of co-education of the colored and white races.

On this point Professor Peabody, of Harvard, remarks: "Of all the experiments in co-education that have been instituted, we regard Berea College, in Kentucky, as the most important in its sphere of influence and in its prophecy of enduring benefit to the colored race. It has carried the war into the enemy's camp, and has brought its whole Christian panoply and armament into the immediate encounter with the surviving spirit of slavery. The college has shown its large educational capacity. Its public exercises have been attended in successive years by persons of established reputation as educationists and literary men, and have received their unqualified commendation and praise. There is, for many miles around, no institution of learning that does nearly so much or so well for its pupils. The consequence is, that those at first vehemently opposed to it are fast falling into the ranks of neutrals or friends. Many who deemed it a nuisance have already sent their children to it. Its sterling value as a seminary of education is now recognized on all hands. But it is of much more worth for its silent yet most efficient propagandism of the due relation between the races; for co-education includes within itself, or involves as its necessary consequence, equality in all civic and social rights, immunities, duties, and obligations. Moreover, a State in which white citizens already seek for their children the privilege of co-education with colored youths, can not long retain its hostility to public schools common to both races. The universal establishment of such schools in the late slave States as we have said, essential to their political and social well-being; and for the advancement of this end Berea College is now doing more than can be effected by any possible legislation, by any action of political parties, or by the combined influence of press, platform, and pulpit."

It is a matter of surprise that so noble and intelligent a State as Kentucky should be far behind other Southern States in its provision for the education of its emancipated citizens.

In South Carolina, Georgia, and Louisiana the law allows no distinction of race, or color, or previous condition. The Legislature of Georgia in 1870 voted an annual appropriation of $8,000 to Atlanta University; the State of Virginia voted a liberal allowance of public money to the Hampton Normal Agricultural Institute; and South Carolina has made a generous appropriation to Claflin University.

With this enlightened policy of other Southern States, it surprises us to find that in Kentucky the colored race have no share of the common-school fund, and are oppressed by peculiar laws. A colored schoolhouse is not allowed within a mile of a white school, nor in towns within six hundred feet. It is forbidden by law for a colored child to attend a white school or a white child a colored school.* President Fairchild says in defense of the co-educatory system of Berea: "We advocate it — 1. Because it is impossible to educate both races separately. In the rural districts it is impossible to maintain two sets of of schools. In the cities it may be done, but in the country it can not. In hundreds of districts there are very few (from five to twenty-five) colored children. They must be admitted to the schools which white children attend, or be left without schools. In other districts the same is true of white children. 2. The separation fosters a spirit of contempt, and haughtiness, and

* These statements are from the report of President Fairchild on Berea College.

182

domineering on the one side, and a sense of debasement and a
spirit of sycophancy or surliness on the other, entirely inconsistent with the highest good of either. It is cruel and abusive
to teach the colored children from the very beginning that they
are only fit for servants of white people, and are not at all to
be tolerated in the same schoolroom with white children. Such
treatment will never make them self-respecting, patriotic,
independent citizens."

It is impossible even to give a minute notice of all the principal universities or colleges that have been established for
the freedmen. But Fiske University, in Nashville, Tennessee,
having a history which has given to it a wide celebrity, we
select that as a specimen of the rest.

From this institution went forth the small band of liberated
slaves called the Jubilee Singers, who conceived the generous
plan of endowing their institution by the exercise of their
musical talent.

Their history is the romance of our period. Starting poor,
simple, unknown, with the disadvantage of their color in their
way, they first gained the ear and heart of the most refined
circles in this country. Crossing the water, they were admitted
to sing before the Queen of England and royal family, and
treated with distinguished hospitality and kindness by the then
Prime Minister, Mr. Gladstone. In Germany they were received with no less consideration by the Emperor and royal
family. In Holland the crowned heads and royal personages
were no less kind, graciously receiving the singers and openly
declaring themselves their patrons. With such patronage their
concerts in all these countries were a brilliant series of tri-
umphs, and Jubilee Hall and Livingstone Hall, with their noble
proportions, and fine architecture, will for ever be a monument
of the success of this simple effort of emancipated slaves.

The catalogue of Fiske University for 1878 gives twenty-six
in the college course, fifty-four in the preparatory department,
twenty-five in the theological course, one hundred and fifty-
three in the normal school course, and eleven in the higher
normal.

The total attendance was three hundred and thirty-eight, of whom one hundred and eighty-one were boarders. Since 1868 regularly trained teachers have been going out from this institution. In 1877 one hundred and five teachers thus prepared were at work in the field of education. Fiske University has also sent out four missionaries to the Mendi mission on the coast of Africa. A deep feeling for mission-work pervades the institution, and ennobles and enlarges the aims of its students, and doubtless others will follow in the steps of those who have so nobly volunteered.

It remains now to speak of those institutions which unite the higher culture of the mind with practical scientific knowledge.

Of these the Hampton Normal and Agricultural Institute, at Hampton, Virginia, is a favorable specimen. This institution was founded ten years ago by the American Missionary Association, and has been aided by the Freedman's bureau and the Peabody Fund, and very largely by individual Christian benevolence. In 1872 the State of Virginia designated Hampton as trustee of that portion of the Agricultural Land Fund which was assigned to the colored people. The amount of $95,000 was invested in State bonds, on which full interest has been paid.

The object of Hampton is to raise up a class of intelligent, cultivated workingmen, to produce thoughtful, intelligent farmers, mechanics, and teachers.

The plan of the Hampton School was suggested by the educational system of the Sandwich Islands, introduced by American missionaries and built up chiefly by the labors of the Rev. Richard Armstrong, D.D., Minister of Public Instruction.

His son, General Armstrong, the Principal of Hampton, inherits and uses to the very best advantage the stores of his father's practical experience.

The following is a list of school industries:

The farm, with bone-grinding, grist-mill, soap-making, blacksmith's shop, butcher's shop, and milk-dairy.

The Engineer's Department, with knitting-machines, broom-shop, shop for iron-work, rag-carpet weaving, and carpenter-shop.

Girls' Industrial Department, for making and mending garments, and learning to sew by hand and machine.

Household work, including washing, ironing, table duty, and cooking-lessons for the girls.

The details for work this year have been as follows:

Girls.—Housework, 98; industrial room, 52; knitting-machine, 21; laundry, 24; weaving rag-carpet, 1; cooking, 20. No work has yet been found for day scholars, 32.

Boys.—Farm, 91; painter, 1; carpenters, 5; broom-making, 2; steam-engine, 1; bone-mill, 2; shoemakers, 4; janitors, 8; knitting-room, 6; blacksmith, 1; office duty, 3; mail-carrier, 1; greenhouse, 1; waiters, 16; laundry, 5; general duty, 5; employed by teachers, 2; day-scholars on orderly duty, 33.

Students' earnings have been as follows:

1875-'76. 101 boys, $5,982.04; 59 girls, $1,647.93; total, $7,629.97.

1876-'77. 125 boys, $7,440.97; 73 girls, $2,139.56; total, $9,580.53.

1877-'78. 138 boys, $11,384.97; 87 girls, $3,046.04; total, $14,431.01.

Average earnings in 1875-'76, boys, $59.23 each; girls, $27.92 each.

Average earnings in 1876-'77, boys, $59.23 each; girls, $29.00 each.

Average earnings in 1877-'78, boys, $82.50 each; girls, $35.01 each.

The problem of the school, industrially, is—

1. To make labor as instructive as possible.

2. To turn it to the best account.

By giving each student one and a half or two days of work each week, and four whole days for study (by having a detail of one fifth out each school day, and all or one half on Saturdays), his mental interests do not suffer materially; he is physi-

cally better off, is able to pay about one half—in some cases
the whole—of his personal expenses, is better fitted to take
care of himself, and becomes more of a man.

Of the results of this school so far, General Armstrong thus
speaks in his last report:

"To the question, 'What becomes of your graduates? we
answer: Not less than ninety per cent. have taught school. We
are satisfied that eighty per cent. were teaching last winter, and
that the large majority will devote themselves to the good of
their people. Those who do not teach are generally working for
themselves or others. I know of but few worthless ones. There
seems to be no general tendency to relapse from the tone given
to their lives at the school. I have observed in many a moral
growth after graduation, the reaction of right life upon character. That some will degenerate there can be no doubt; but,
after leaving here, the general movement is upward.

"The little army of Hampton's graduates is becoming a
power. For the first time in the school's history they have, this
year, an alumni meeting. Their union and mutual sympathy,
and their relations with the school, are of great importance. To
many, the school is their only home. It is the birthplace of their
better life; and they give to it an affection and confidence that
create an obligation on our part.

"This year the newspapers of the school reading-room have,
after lying a week on the table, been distributed among graduates in every direction, also quantities of illustrated papers;
many have been given by friends of the school for this purpose.
They have received much benefit from the State 'Educational
Journal' which is sent to them. Next year we intend to have a
graduate department; making as complete a record of them as
possible, corresponding with each one, supplying good reading matter, of which they are often destitute, thus keeping
them in pleasant and close relations with us, and encouraging
and cheering them in every possible way. By such moral support they will be stronger, better, safer. Thus will the result of
our labor be preserved, and a guild of earnest, high-minded,
united, and powerful workers be formed as a nucleus of civili-

zation, a barrier to the mischievous element among their people, and, in connection with a similar class from other institutions, become a basis of hope for the race; they will be civilizers rather than mere pedagogues; the future leaders of their race, and occupy a place not yet taken."

The institution publishes a paper called "The Southern Workman," which has a large circulation and is a most valuable and efficient means of continuing its good influences over those who have left. Its practical essays on the subject of health, cleanliness, ventilation, drainage, and general hygiene, have been so valuable that a series of them called "Hampton Tracts" have been extensively circulated and recommended in Northern States.

The printing and press-work is entirely done in the institution, and furnishes one more useful trade for those who are employed in it.

A similar work to that of Hampton is being done at Claflin University, Orangeburg, South Carolina, and at Talladega College, Alabama, and at Tongaloo University, Mississippi. There is also the beginning of an agricultural department announced in connection with Atlanta University, Georgia, to which the Legislature of the State has made an appropriation of $8,000 per annum.

The last and most significant item in our review of the tableau of educational effort among the freedmen is the increasingly friendly attitude of most of the Southern States toward this enterprise.

We have purposely omitted to dwell on those exhibitions of bitterness and violence which often marked the commencement of these educational enterprises at the South. It is due to the intelligent Southerners to admit that such violence proceeded mostly from the uncultivated classes, and that everywhere through the South *educated* men have been prompt to feel the imperative need of culture for the enfranchised slaves.

In 1871 the Commissioners appointed by the State of Georgia attended the annual examination at Atlanta University. The report of this Committee, signed by ex-Governor J. E. Brown, thus speaks: "At every step of the examination we were impressed with the fallacy of the popular idea (which, in common with thousands of others, a majority of the undersigned have heretofore entertained) that the members of the African race are not capable of a high grade of intellectual culture. The rigid tests to which the classes in algebra and geometry, and in Latin and Greek, were subjected, unequivocally demonstrated that, under judicious training and with persevering study, there are many members of the African race who can attain a high grade of intellectual culture. They prove that they can master intricate problems in mathematics, and fully comprehend the construction of difficult passages in the classics.

"Many of the pupils exhibited a degree of mental culture which, considering the length of time their minds have been in training, would do credit to members of any race."

Dr. Cooke, President of Claflin University, writes us that both Governor Wade Hampton and Mayor H. S. Thomson, State Superintendent of Education in South Carolina, attended their late commencement and addressed words of encouragement to all interested in the advance of the institution. Two appropriations of $7,500 have been made to the institution since Governor Hampton took the chair.

General Armstrong, of Hampton, remarks on this subject:

"Our relations with the State of Virginia, as trustee of that part of the land fund devoted to the colored people, have been in all ways satisfactory. Interest has been promptly paid. Throughout the State the feeling is kindly and encouraging to to good work for the negro race.

"During the past ten years there has been a progress in Southern sentiment, in respect to the negro, readily apparent only to those who can look behind the front presented by politicians and periodicals. Thought, experience, and necessity have pushed out old ideas and pushed up new ones. The change has been, I believe, as great as was possible for human nature under the circumstances, and in time will be so regarded. Other lines than those of race are being drawn. Common sense and common interest are working against deeply seated notions and prejudices that will yield because weak in themselves, and because they do not pay."

The Hon. Robert M. Lusher, State Superintendent of Education in Louisiana, uses this noble language: "It is with the aid of education alone, finally, that patriots can hope to see the vexed question of the harmonious relation between the two races settled—with no humiliation to the higher, with no degradation to the humbler. This question is, indeed, one that trenches upon the imminent present. For good or evil, a race equal to the whites—at least in numbers—passing suddenly from a condition of slavery to a condition of freedom, continuing and needed to continue in its former home, must assert itself. It should be the duty—as it is clearly the interest—of the State to see that that race shall assert itself in knowledge—not in ignorance; in a loyal understanding of its obligations—not in a blind disregard of them; in an intelligent participation hereafter in the responsible duties of American citizenship . . . . If the next colored generations, then, are to consist of good citizens, not weak tools for designing politicians, they should be educated. If they are to be conservative American citizens, lending their aid alike to the progress of the State and to the advancement of the public, they should be educated. If they are to make common accord with the whites, only recognizing in the latter the superiority that lies in lineage and in noble memories, indissolubly connected with the history of the world's most exalted civilization; and if they are to work with these, with good heart and earnest endeavor, to a common patriotic end, they must be taught that their State has no preferences, but that, like a kindly mother, she gathers in her tender bosom all the children who owe their existence to her."

In the State where the author now has a home, Governor Drew, in his first message to the Legislature of Florida, uses this language in relation to the education of the freedmen: "Now that a very large constituent element of our population is released from bondage and intrusted with the power of the ballot, a system of free schools has become a means of self-preservation. To educate the colored race and fit them to exercise the privilege of voting intelligently—to perform all the sacred duties of freemen, to enjoy their liberty, to become wise and good citizens—imposes upon us a task to perform, a responsibility from which we can not escape. Then let us set about the work cheerfully."

The author can bear testimony, so far as personal observation goes, that the government of the State of Florida is administered in this spirit.

Before coming to the close of this article, one acknowledgment—one tribute of admiration—is here due to the agency of a noble man, who, though dead, has been living to a most glorious purpose in this work of Southern reorganization. The Peabody fund, amounting to millions of dollars, has been a constant factor in all the good accomplished. Its agent has administered this delicate and difficult trust with an energy, a wisdom, an impartiality, that lead us to feel that the Father of Lights must have imparted to him divine guidance. In all the reports we have examined we meet everywhere the traces of this noble charity, administered with such timely wisdom as to double the value of every sum contributed. America will long have reason to bless God for the bequest of Peabody, and for the administration of Dr. Sears.

Thus have we given a very imperfect summary of the lasting results which have followed a great educational enthusiasm— a great national reconstruction.

Is not this army of schools and colleges—this educational impulse pervading society—a better guarantee for the future than *any* ignoble party strife?

And if our national Government should grant to the impoverished Southern States the funds they ask to carry through a universal system of education, would it not be an investment which would yield the nation a thousand-fold in return?

Class prejudices can not be *legislated* away, but they can be educated away. This noble system of common schools, colleges, and industrial institutes now rising at the South, if re-enforced by national grants, would in a few years regenerate society, and entirely prevent the possibility of such struggles as have lately dishonored the voting-places of the United States.

Education will bring quiet, refinement, respect for law, respect for the mutual rights of races; and America, where so many races meet and mingle, will be the true millennial ground, where the fatherhood of God is shown in the brotherhood of man.

11

Chautauqua Local Circles and Summer Assemblies

Anonymous

Two thousand and more Local Circles of the Chautauqua Literary and Scientific Circle will be in course of organization —or re-organization—when this issue of *The Chautauquan* reaches its readers. The purpose and plan of each are matters for serious consideration, for without an honest determined purpose to do thorough intellectual work, the best plans will "gang a-gley"; without a suitable plan, the noblest purpose will be fruitless. The first is matter for the individual members. They alone can resolve. The foundation for the second may come from anybody within or without, but it must be molded to suit the peculiar need of the body which is to use it. No two circles are exactly alike, and when one adopts another's suggestions it must make them *fit*. With this understanding the Scribe ventures on two or three hints for the coming year.

The first of these is an ambitious one, but there are many circles which are able to accomplish ambitious things. It is that in those circles—and they are many—where the plan is adopted of taking up one subject only of the course for circle work, that a series of special lectures on the subject follow the discussion of the textbook. This suggestion has been made before in *The Chautauquan*, but no lecture bureau has existed to which circles could be referred for obtaining material for

Reprinted from *The Chautauquan*, Vol. 10, No. 1, Oct. 1889, pp. 102-113.

such special work. This difficulty has been conquered. Chautauqua has added to her many-halled structure an English plan for carrying University-instruction to the people, known as the University-Extension Scheme. The methods of work in this scheme are thus described in the prospectus which the committee recently has issued:

1. University-Extension work will be under the management and supervision of a Central Committee, who are advised and assisted by a General Committee selected from representative College and University Professors, who will nominate candidates for itinerant lectureships from among the younger specialists who are personally known to be fitted for the task of popular teaching. A faculty of University-Extension Lecturers will be gradually formed, from which local demands for lecture courses will be supplied when possible.

2. The courses consist of twelve weekly lectures, each occupying about an hour. For about three-quarters of an hour, preceding or following each lecture, a class is held for those students who wish to study the subject more thoroughly. The object of the class is to give the students an opportunity of coming into personal contact with the lecturer, in order that they may, by conversation and discussion with him, the better familiarize their minds with the principles of the subject, and get their special difficulties explained. The teaching in the class is conversational.

3. In order to enable the students to follow the lecture readily, and to carry away the substance of it, a printed Syllabus, usually in pamphlet form and interleaved, is prepared beforehand by the lecturer for the use of his students.

4. Printed questions are provided for each lecture, which may be answered by the students in writing at home, and submitted to the lecturer for correction and comment.

5. At the end of the course an examination is held, under the authority of the Central Committee, and only those students are admitted to the examination who have attended the lectures and classes to the satisfaction of the lecturer, and have done such an amount of weekly exercises as the lecturer may

have required. The examination is not compulsory, but it is desirable that as many students as possible should present themselves.

The advantage to a circle of such a lecture course need not be emphasized. But it should not be undertaken until a careful study of the text-book has been made. The way to go to work to arrange for a course, the cost, and who can be obtained, may be learned by addressing *Frederick Starr, Secretary, New Haven, Conn.* Something can be learned, too, by pondering the experience of a circle of C.L.S.C. graduates in Portage, Wisconsin. These graduates organized last fall a separate circle, and took up the study of Germany — its history, literature, art, biography, and geography. Topics for study were carefully arranged in advance, and printed upon a leaflet with desirable books of reference. A course of stereopticon lectures was suggested as an aid to study, and almost unawares the society found itself carrying out a broad educational scheme which embraced a large portion of the intelligent part of the community. The Opera House was secured for a course of lectures, a stereopticon and slides were rented, and all available local talent, clergymen, lawyers, and teachers of the city pressed into the service as lecturers. Season tickets were sold at a dollar each, entitling the holder to twenty lectures illustrated by from twenty to fifty views, at an expense of five cents for each lecture. Single tickets were sold at fifty cents each, and though the expense of the course amounted to nearly four hundred dollars, the circle closed the season free of debt. Increased interest in the lectures was manifested as the season advanced, and many weary and burdened men and women came to look forward to the lecture evening as the one bright spot in their lives. The influence upon the community was very marked, and the members of the circle were so encouraged by their success that a similar plan for the study of the British Isles has been suggested for this year. The undergraduate circle worked heartily with their comrades in pushing the enterprise, at the same time keeping up their regular meetings, while the graduates met once a week and studied up the topic for the coming lecture. It was a fine example of what co-operation will do.

Current news and fresh matter bearing on the readings are always a help to a circle, and a systematic plan for gathering and presenting such items will be found advantageous. The Scribe knows of no better plan than to keep on one's reading table a quantity of thin paste-board cards about 5x2 inches in size and ruled with a red line 1½ inches from the end. In reading, use these cards for taking notes. Thus the circle is reading Political Economy and the principle of co-operation is before it. A member finds a report from the Pillsbury Mills in Minneapolis showing how co-operation worked there in the last year. He cuts it out for his scrap-book, and on a note-card writes:

Co-operation. See Scrap-book. Page _____.	Report of Pillsbury Mills in Minneapolis for year 1889.

In a month he will accumulate several of these notes on co-operation. He can then put his material together in a paper or a verbal report and carry it to the circle. The cards should be saved and arranged in alphabetical order. References to points in books can be easily found in this manner. Where the book is not one's own the particular point can be copied into a blank book (every reader should own such a book for saving matter, just as he should own a scrap-book). Matter will accumulate pertaining to every subject which comes before the circle, and the half-hour devoted to a report of what the members have picked up during the week, of current news bearing on the subjects in their course, will become one of the brightest and most profitable of the meetings.

The attention which will be given to art in the coming year opens a fine opportunity for the illustrated scrap-book maker. The better class of illustrated newspapers print wood-cuts of the best pictures at every French *salon* and English and American exhibition, and by saving these with the explanation attached, a good idea of the best pictures of the day and familiarty with artists can be obtained. Illustrated catalogues of the expositions are also obtainable at a small cost. Illustrated magazine articles on the works of the old masters are not hard to secure. Indeed by thrift and ingenuity a very complete and respectable art collection can be made.

The department of Local Work will be continued during the year under Local Circles. Last year most of the reports were on Local Charities. The range, however, is not limited. Local Dialect, History, Charities, and Laws are all welcome. Many readers in following Prof. Shaler's studies of the physiography of the fields about him, will gather interesting notes on plants, animals, and the soil. These very properly belong to Local Studies and will be given a place there if sent to *The Chautauquan.*

A charming example of what one may do in local work, in even so narrow a limit as one's door-yard, was shown the Scribe last summer at Chautauqua in the class cottage of the Irrepressibles. From an '84 in Hiawatha, Kansas, had come a herbarium of the flowers — wild and cultivated — in her garden. The portfolio contained some seventy-five specimens beautifully mounted on separate sheets. It was a delightful souvenir for the class and a stimulating example to those who realizing that their range in the world is narrow, would get as much from it as if it were wide.

The number of local circles made up of graduates of the Chautauqua Literary and Scientific Circle has led to the arrangement of a special course for them. The "General Announcement" sent from the Plainfield Office says: "The plan of study of the Chautauqua Literary and Scientific Circle embodies two elements: first, a preliminary four years' course in science and general literature, designed to give, in some degree, the general college outlook; and second, advanced work in special lines, to be continued as long as the student desires to work under the direction of his *alma mater.* The first part of this plan has been developed with marked success, and with the close of the year 1889 the graduates of the Chautauqua Circle will number more than twenty thousand.

Many of these students have already taken up special lines of work, but it is believed that this graduates' organization is now strong enough to support a definite course of advanced study, and that the necessary development of the higher work of the C. L. S. C. demands special provision for this need. The Chautauqua Circle therefore offers a special advanced three years' course in English History and Literature. This course is intended for all graduates, but those who prefer other lines of work will have the privilege of choosing, as heretofore, from the Seal courses given in the C.L.S.C. hand-book. This three years' course will be followed by similar courses in other subjects. The plan is to mark out a three years' course in the history and literature of England, to specify the books required, to expand the course by recommending other books for those who have much time, to furnish helps and suggestions by instructors who are specialists in their departments, to make full tests and reviews, and to adapt the course and suggestions to circle work. The readings of each year will be so arranged that graduates of later classes will be able to fall in with the work of the year then current. The course in general will be adapted (1) to those who wish simply to read; (2) to those who have time and inclination for thorough study." The directors of the course are, in History, Prof. H. B. Adams, Ph. D., of Johns Hopkins University, and in Literature, Prof. W. D. McClintock, A. M., of Chautauqua College.

The readings for the coming year include Green's "Short History of the English People"; Stubbs' "Early Plantaganets"; Poole's "Wycliffe and Movements for Reform"; Ward's "English Poets"; "Typical Selections from English Prose Writers"; Introduction to Minto's "Manual of English Prose Literature"; Scott's "Ivanhoe"; The Chautauquan, which will contain special required articles.

This course will be welcomed, we are confident, by many circles. The Graduate Circles will be given a department in *Local Circles,* their reports appearing together, as do those of Chautauqua Literary and Scientific Circle.

It has been customary in local circles to celebrate certain

special occasions called Memorial Days. At the head of this department a list of the fixed Memorial Days stands from month to month. The list also contains two special Memorial Days chosen from the names of those persons who are particularly celebrated in the subject which is most prominent in the readings. Thus for the present month Adam Smith is suggested, because of the place Political Economy takes in the month's reading. Next month we shall have a Romulus Day; in December a Brutus Day; and so through the year. This gives circles a subject for an entertainment or special program without taking them too far from their readings. To aid in preparing for these Days, the *Suggestive Programs* will always contain something suitable for the occasion, and in *The Question Table* will be found a set of questions calling out the leading points in the man's life. It must not be concluded that because so many Days are proposed, circles are supposed to celebrate all or even a majority of them; one or two celebrations in a year, carefully planned and executed, are worth more than a dozen inferior ones. The Logansport, Indiana, Circle did a much more valuable piece of work last year in their "Penelope's Symposium" than if they had held monthly unimportant celebrations; that is, one "big thing" is worthy several small ones. It will be found a good rule for circles to observe only such special occasions as their time and taste enable them to observe on a generous scale and with hearty co-operation.

THE SUMMER ASSEMBLIES.

Chautauqua, New York. A retrospect of the sixteenth Chautauqua session is a pleasant and inspiring task. The opening—July 2— was encouraging Those present remarked after a first walk, "How things are improved!"—and they were. The grounds were clean, flowers, walks, and shrubbery were in good condition, new and elegant cottages and improved old ones were conspicuous, a large and elegant new office building devoted to The Chautauquan and the *Assembly Daily Herald* was a marked improvement, the Kellogg Memorial Building, built by Mr. J. H. Kellogg, of Troy, N. Y., in honor of his mother, made a fine addition to the more pretentious architecture of the grounds and gave excellent accommodations to the various departments of children's work, to the art and industrial classes, and to the Woman's Christian Temperance Union. Chautauqua beamed with beauty and fresh attractions. Those for whom all this had been prepared, responded generously. July has been considered the quiet month of the season, but this year it was difficult to distinguish it from August. The cottages were all open and the boarding places and hotels full. In whatever way measured, the attendance was unprecedented.

The surprising increase in attendance was well illustrated in the College where over five hundred students were enrolled, nearly forty per cent more than in any previous year. This enrollment had a wide territorial variety, thirty-five states being represented, twelve students coming from Canada, two from China, and one from Bulgaria. The prosperity of the college had other signs than numbers; one of them was the growth of the reference library. Over one thousand volumes are now on the shelves, and the beginning of a library fund has been made by a generous friend from Illinois, who has placed a considerable sum at the disposal of the college to be used for historical works. The Museum has grown so that it was possible to use it largely this summer in illustrating historical lectures. The rare lot of antiquities received from the Egypt Exploration Fund through Miss Amelia B. Edwards was particularly valuable. The splendid teaching force was at its best and was made still stronger than had been promised, by drafting into service during their visits many eminent lecturers, notably the distinguished foreign guest of the Assembly, Prof. J. P. Mahaffy of Dublin University—who during his visit devoted an hour each day to a Greek class, the Alcestis of Euripides being read. The enthusiasm and self-congratulation with which the College body closed the season was entirely justified. The session was in every respect remarkable.

The Rev. A. E. Winship, editor of the New England *Journal of Education,* remarked while at Chautauqua, "The summer school life promises to be as much a benefit to the schools as the introduction of the normal school. Many towns raise the pay of those teachers so much per month for the year who attend summer schools. Other school boards pass a vote in commendation of the teachers who attend, putting their names on record." The attendance at the Teachers' Retreat was a proof that Mr. Winship's theory is believed by teachers — and a sign too of the high regard in which they hold Dr. Dickinson and his assistants' work at Chautauqua, for it never before was so large — three hundred eighty-four persons being enrolled. The usual work on pedagogy was done. An especially delightful feature of the Retreat was the Tourist's Conferences conducted by Mr. G. E. Vincent.

The elaborate platform work announced in the spring issues of this magazine was carried out almost without a break — a great feat of organizing and executive ability. The credit of the program and its execution are largely due to Mr. Geo. E. Vincent, Chancellor Vincent's son, popularly known as George I. Mr. Vincent really holds the position of vice-chancellor at Chautauqua. His ideas for the Assembly are always high and advanced. His insight into popular taste and a student's needs is keen and correct, and he has the executive force to carry out what he attempts. The most interesting and suggestive feature of the lecture season was the tendency to lecture courses and the evident satisfaction the thoughtful listeners took in this arrangement. Several notable series were delivered by eminent persons, including Donald G. Mitchell, H. H. Boyesen, Miss Mary E. Beedy, Dr. H. B. Adams, Dr. F. W. Gunsaulus, Dr. R. T. Ely, Miss Jane Meade Welch, Prof. J. P. Mahaffy, and Washington Gladden. The opportunity this gave for following through several days the development of a line of strong thought by one man — and that one eminent as a scholar and man of achievements — was heartily appreciated. Prof. Ely's course was conducted on the University-Extension plan, a syllabus of each lecture appearing beforehand in the *Assembly Herald* and an examination being conducted at the close. The lighter platform work was excellent. The plan inaugurated last year of putting on an entertainment each day was continued this year, and a concert, reading, or stereopticon lecture relieved the serious daily work. One brilliant entertainment not advertised beforehand occurred the night of August 30, a fire which swept away a block of buildings owned by the Assembly. The fact that the fire did not spread and that there was no loss of life or limb caused more rejoicing over the escape than regret over the loss. The Great Days of the year were immense successes — characterized by great crowds, great speeches, and great fun.

The most ambitious new feature of the season was the school of Music. The result justified the pains taken to organize this school. In class work all departments of Vocal Music, not only voice culture, reading, sight-singing, but also composition in music and harmony were included. Elocution, as it applies to music, was taught by Prof. Cumnock. The Normal department instructed those who teach in public schools and elsewhere. Private lessons were given by such eminent specialists as Profs. Ellis, Wheeler, Flagler, Sherwood, and Palmer. The music at the Amphitheater was in itself so good that it was an education. On especial advantage was the presence of that almost faultless pianist, Mr. W. H. Sherwood, whose recitals created great enthusiasm. The number of public readings was increased though it would not be possible to improve the quality. Besides Prof. Cumnock, Messrs. Cable, Riddle, and Burbank, who have read before at Chautauqua, Richard Malcolm Johnston and Leland Powers were present.

The Chautauqua Literary and Scientific Circle was an active force throughout the entire two months, and during the weeks of the Assembly proper from August 6-27, it carried everything before it. Great numbers of members were present, many circles sending representatives, and many clubs and excursions coming; the largest of these was the Brooklyn Assembly excursion composed of some three hundred C. L. S. C. members. Class Headquarters were opened promptly and the whole number from '82 to '93 were thoroughly organized for social enjoyment and C. L. S. C. agitation. The eve of Recognition Day was taken for class receptions. A more delightful custom could not be imagined. Each class was the center of a thoroughly congenial and happy company of classmates. During the evening Chancellor Vincent and Principal Hurlbut with their wives and a few others interested in the C. L. S. C. made the rounds of the receptions, at each leaving a few words of congratulation and encouragement. The great success of this Reception evening ought to lead to its incorporation into the festivities of Recognition Day. Of that day it is hardly necessary to speak. It was as always full of the best things and ended with a new feature, a banquet for members of the S. H. G. This idea comes from the Framingham Assembly where the graduate banquet for several years has been a feature of Recognition Day.

The social side of all departments of Chautauqua life was noticeably quickened. This came largely from the fact that as years go by, each particular interest is gathering close to it more and more who are in sympathy with its object and who draw in others. The increasing number of "headquarters" help social life no little. The recognition of this fact is leading to the establishment of large numbers of such places. The Presbyterians have taken steps to erect a building before the coming season—and it will probably be in stone. The Episcopalians started a building fund, which grew sufficiently to warrant the beginning of a building. Another year will see probably the new Union Class Building for the C.L.S.C. and a chapel for the college. One of the best results of this increase in accommodations will be the increase in social life.

With all the hard work of the Assembly there was large attention given to wholesome, out-of-door life. The classes in Physical Culture were never so large and the department was strengthened by adding instructors in the Delsarte system, in Swedish exercises, and in swimming. Tennis and base ball "raged"; the tournaments and matched games being as popular as Gunsaulus himself. The authorities at Chautauqua, believe thoroughly in the "Gospel of fresh air" and are striving to provide such a variety of intelligent sports that nobody will have an excuse for omitting daily exercise.

Under all the diversified interests of the great Assembly was a deep, genuine spirituality. The work was all pre-eminently God's work. Prof. Mahaffy said in a Sunday evening talk to a great Amphitheater audience, "I asked to do only one thing when I consented to come to Chautauqua—to speak once on a religious theme." Like him the workers of the entire force asked one thing before anything else, each to put the stamp of religion on his work. Dr. Dunning said in talking of the movement, "The heart of Chautauqua is the study of the Bible." It has never been so true as now, for never has so much and so intelligent thought been given to the place the Bible shall occupy in the Chautauqua Movement.

Bay View, Michigan. The fourteenth Bay View season is reported the largest and most successful ever known at that favored place. It opened on July 16 and closed August 14, and Assembly workers of wide acquaintance, who were there, commented on its completeness and excellence. Its public buildings are built for permanence, and are admirably planned, home-like, and elegant. Indeed the entire place has the appearance of a solid, well-built summer city of three hundred fifty cottages. Bay View is in a thrifty condition. Wild and expensive schemes have been avoided and a good credit maintained from the outset.

This year the erection of Hitchcock Hall, the finest building for the purpose at any Assembly, gave impetus to the Sunday-school Normal department in charge of the Rev. Horace Hitchcock, of Detroit. A fine public library and museum were also added this year, and for next season a $5,000 W. C. T. U. building, the gift of Mrs. R. G. Peters, of Manistee, is announced.

Of the nine departments in the Bay View Summer University, foremost has been the Literary department with sixteen courses, large attendance, and the highest order of work, under

Prof. David Howell. Another decided success was the new School of English Bible, and an advance step has been the unification with it of all classes in Bible instruction, from the children's classes upward.

The C. L. S. C. meetings were a prominent feature all the season. Daily Round Tables and other characteristic meetings filled the 5 o'clock hour, and the beautiful Chautauqua cottage was always a popular resort.

Recognition Day was a notable occasion, and thirty-five diplomas were delivered. President L. R. Fiske, of Albion College, gave the address. The Rev. Dr. James A. Worden stated from the platform that he had been to thirty Assemblies, and the general program at Bay View was as complete, varied, and as fine as any seen.

Drs. Gunsaulus and Henson were there, and so were Miss Frances Willard and Mrs. Angie F. Newman, Mr. Leland Powers, Frank Beard, Philip Phillips, Prof. E. E. White, Prof. J. B. DeMotte, the Rev. Dr. S. L. Baldwin, Mrs. S. M. I. Henry, the Rev. J. A. Worden, Mr. C. E. Bolton, and Prof. C. C. Case in charge of music, Mrs. Alice J. Osborne, soloist, from Boston, and the Alma Band.

A W. C. T. U. School of Methods with eminent workers in charge, ran through one full week, and likewise a Missionary Institute with signal success.

It is said that although Michigan is one of the smallest states in population, it leads all others in Chautauqua work, in proportion to population, having nearly one-fifteenth of all the Chautauquans. This is in a large measure due to the energy of Mr. John M. Hall, of Flint, Michigan. Mr. Hall paid the original Chautauqua a visit after the close of this year's session, that he might catch whatever new ideas were to be found there.

Beatrice, Nebraska. The first meeting of the Beatrice Assembly closed July 8 after a session of ten days. From the beginning to the end it was a demonstration of what energy and enterprise can accomplish. The many who were present went away only to speak in its praise, and its success predicts still greater success for future years. To those having the matter in charge great credit is due for the fine program presented both as regards lecturers and instructors.

Beatrice is one of the most enterprising and beautiful young cities of south-east Nebraska. On the banks of the Big Blue River, a mile or less from the city, is a fine park of ninety acres which has been dedicated to the intellectual, religious, and moral advancement of the people. A Tabernacle capable of seating 3,000 people, three excellent study halls, a dining-hall, and tent accommodations for 2,000 people, with other accommodations in abundance, represent the amplitude of the provision made for the outer man.

Dr. John E. Earp, president of the South-west Kansas College, was Superintendent of Instruction and teacher of the Senior Normal class. He succeeded in placing over the various departments of instruction capable teachers who held the interest of the classes throughout the session. In the music presented, the young city showed that it possessed talent of a high order.

The platform talent was represented by Dr. J. B. DeMotte, Dr. G. W. Miller, Dr. J. B. Young, Dr. Geo. P. Hays, Peter M. Von Finkelstein, Dr. Creighton, Robert McIntyre, Sam P. Jones, Dr. H. D. Fisher, and others, representing several social and religious organizations, of special excellence in their several lines of work.

July 5 was Recognition Day, on which occasion seven graduates, after passing through the Golden Gate, received their diplomas. Addresses were made to the class by Dr. Young and Dr. George P. Hays. The day closed with a Camp-Fire, around which a circle was formed and a praise service held.

Connecticut Valley, Northampton, Mass. For the benefit of the many who were debarred from attending any of the regular Assemblies, a few active and earnest men planned a Chautauqua gathering for the western part of Massachusetts. The first session was held at Laurel Park, Northampton, in

1887, and was a success. The second in 1888, met with a still better reception. And the third, from July 17-24, has just closed with larger receipts than ever before, and with bright prospects for its future career.

The lecture platform for the present year needs no comments since it comprised such men as Geo. Makepeace Towle, Robert Nourse, C. E. Bolton with stereopticon, J. H. Mansfield, Charles Parkhurst, Pleasant Hunter, C. T. Winchester, Alexander McKenzie, all with their D. D.'s and other honorable titles. Moreover the directors were peculiarly fortunate in having in their own body minute-men fully able to meet any emergency. If any advertised lecturer was compelled at the last moment to cancel his engagement, Prof. Pillsbury, of Smith College fame, stepped in and made up the deficiency.

The Normal Hour, Teachers' classes, Recognition Day, Temperance Day, with evening bells and concerts and fireworks, gave a taste to all in the western part of the state, of the original article, with all the flavor and freshness pertaining to youth.

In the entire management of the undertaking the Rev. George H. Clark, President, and the Rev. George H. Johnson, Treasurer, proved themselves practical business men, and to them the Assembly feels greatly indebted. All interested wish to join in efforts to make this newcomer in the list of Assemblies a worthy associate of all her older sisters.

Council Bluffs and Omaha, Iowa. The reports from the first session of the Council Bluffs and Omaha Assemblies, held June 13 to July 4, are most encouraging. All feel assured that its good success leaves no doubt as to the permanency of the institution. The management was pronounced excellent, nothing having been left undone which could add to the comfort and the pleasure of the visitor. The location is all that could be desired, and the large grounds comprising 127 acres are finely laid out and finely kept.

Among the speakers who helped make the program, as it was reported "the best possible to be devised," were the Hon.

Will Cumback, Frank Beard, Peter Von Finkelstein, Prof. Cooper, Dr. Donald Macrae, Dr. George P. Hays, the Hon. G. W. Bain, Dr. W. L. Davidson. The beautiful and commodious Amphitheater, which has a seating capacity of 6,000, was often put to a test to provide room for all who wished to hear the entertainments offered. Among special days during the session were Temperance Day, Independence Day, and Grand Army Day, all of which were celebrated with imposing services.

On Recognition Day, June 24, the usual exercises were observed and diplomas were presented to ten graduates. As is always the case, this was looked upon as the great day of the season, and enthusiastic Chautauquans, auguring from its success and delights, look forward to its arrival in future years with hope. Larger classes will be expected on each ensuing year.

Dr. Gillet, the Superintendent of Instruction, made at the close the following statement of the number of classes, entertainments, etc., that have been enjoyed by the Chautauqua visitors this season. The summary is as follows: fifty-one lectures, fifteen sessions of first year Normal class, thirty sessions of Boys and Girls' class, thirty chorus rehearsals, eleven Assembly Bible class meetings, eleven meetings of Greek class, ten meetings of Voice Culture class, eighteen meetings of Elocution class, thirty Concerts, five Literary lectures, eight Medical lectures, fourteen meetings of C. L. S. C., two Vesper meetings.

At the final meeting of the C. L. S. C. Round Table, a branch of the Council Bluffs and Omaha Assembly was formed, composed of four officers, seven executives, one organizing secretary, and thirty county secretaries. It is to be the work of this branch assembly to organize local circles throughout the adjacent towns and townships. A resolution also passed by this executive committee to aid, in every way possible, its Chautauqua Assembly.

Crete, Nebraska. Before the eighth annual session of the Crete Assembly had closed, active preparations were making for the ninth—a fact which tells the whole story as to the successful outcome of the present season. The Assembly opened on June 27 and for the thirteen days of its continuance all those present congratulated themselves on their good fortune in being there. The platform program is pronounced the most superior in every respect of any yet presented. The music under Dr. Palmer more than met even the high expectations regarding it. And in all of the Chautauqua work proper—the Sunday-school and C. L. S. C. departments which form the foundation of the entire enterprise—the highest satisfaction was expressed. Dr. Dunning as Superintendent of Instruction kept every part of the work well manned and spared no pains in order that all requirements should be met.

Among the propositions made for the next session was one for holding a Teachers' Retreat of two or three weeks. It met with general favor and may be regarded as one of the regular features of the Assembly hereafter. A committee, consisting of Dr. Duryea, President Foss, Prof. Sweezey, and Prof. Bessey, was appointed to arrange a course of study and provide instruction.

On Recognition Day thirteen graduates passed through with the customary regulations and received the C. L. S. C. diplomas. A finely adapted address was made to the class by Dr. Alexander McKenzie, of Harvard University. Much enthusiasm was shown in the organization of the Class of '93. The Chautauqua spirit proved contagious and over fifty names were enrolled, with the prospect of a large increase.

Island Park, Indiana. The eleventh session of this Assembly was held July 31 to August 12. There was a larger daily attendance, probably by one-third, than at any former Assembly. This gave not only encouragement to the management, but an inspiration to all the workers, both on the platform and in the classes. The devotional meetings each morning were seasons of great religious interest, and were well attended by the residents. The Class Department was characterized by large attendance and intense interest.

Dr. M. M. Parkhurst daily conducted the Mininsters' Institute; Mrs. D. B. Wells and Miss C. B. Sharp, the Woman's Work Institute; Dr. A. C. Barnes, the Chautauqua Normal; and the Rev. J. E. Irvin and Miss Lura Love, the Boys and Girls' class. The special classes were: Kindergarten, taught by Miss Lottie Daniels; Physical Culture, Miss M. Scidmore; Wood-carving, Miss Dill; and Painting in oil, Mrs. C. B. Hare. The platform was a scene of continual attraction. The Otsego Cornet Band discoursed first-class music. Its reputation led to great expectations, and the audience was not disappointed. Prof. S. H. Blakeslee, music director, has few equals. The concerts he gave with the special talent, assisted by his large chorus, were complimentary to his ability as an organizer and instructor.

Lectures were delivered by Joseph Cook, Gen. O. O. Howard, Gen. W. H. Gibson, Sam W. Small, M. M. Parkhurst, L. A. Belt, A. J. Fish, R. M. Barns, Geo. P. Hays, J. A. P. McGaw, Prof. J. B. DeMotte, Prof. C. E. Stokes, Francis Murphy, A. C. Barnes, T. C. Read, Professor Underhill, Dr. J. B. Stemen, H. S. Gekler, T. C. Jackson, and others.

The great days were Grand Army with Generals Howard and Gibson speakers; W. C. T. U. Day, with Sam W. Small and A. J. Fish; and Temperance Day, with Francis Murphy, Generals Howard and Gibson, and A. C. Barnes.

Recognition Day was unusually interesting. The attendance was very large, many members of the C. L. S. C. being present from Indiana, Michigan, and Ohio. The orators of the day were Dr. Geo. P. Hays and Dr. C. H. Payne. Eleven graduates received their diplomas at the hands of the superintendent, the Rev. N. B. C. Love, who presented them with well chosen words.

A Union C. L. S. C. organization was perfected; and thorough work in the interests of the C. L. S. C. will be done in the patronizing territory of this Assembly.

Already the program for 1890 is being prepared. The Rev. N. B. C. Love holds the positions of President and Superintendent of Instruction, and he has been secured in the same positions the ensuing year. The Rev. L. J. Naftzger, the Secretary and Assistant Superintendent, has done excellent service, and will retain his positions another year. The management is congratulating itself upon its financial success this year. The receipts very considerably exceed the expenditures, and there is great hopefulness for the future.

Topeka, Kansas. A most attractive program was presented at the Kansas Assembly during its session from June 25 to July 4. The lecture corps included Bishops Vincent and Ninde, Robert McIntyre, the Rev. Drs. Geo. C. Lorimer, J.L. Hurlbut, Wm. Butler, G.W. Miller, J.B. Young, President McVicar, of Washburn College, and other well-known speakers.

June 27, Recognition Day, found over 10,000 people on the Assembly grounds. The C.L.S.C. procession escorted to the Golden Gate the graduates who then passed through the Arches to the Hall of Philosophy for formal Recognition by Chancellor Vincent. Passing next to the Tabernacle, the address to the graduates was delivered by Bishop Vincent, and fifty-five diplomas were conferred. Many of these diplomas were well decorated with seals, one alone bearing twenty-eight. A Camp-Fire and a "ghost procession" were features of the evening.

June 29 was Oxford League Day, and July 2 was devoted to the interests of children. The orators on Independence Day were Dr. Jesse Bowman Young, who gave "Chapters from a Story: What a Boy saw in the Army," Robert McIntyre, whose subject was "The Iliad of America," and Dr. G. W. Miller, who told some of his experiences in the "Shadows and Sunshine of the War."

The special classes were well attended. They included Sunday-school Normal, Greek, Oratory, and Vocal and Instrumental Music. Woman's missionary work was a prominent feature of the Assembly. This department was in charge of Mrs. Bishop Ninde, assisted by active leaders in home and foreign fields.

Lake Bluff, Illinois. The Assembly—July 24 to Aug. 6—was a success. Hitherto not much stress has been laid upon the

Chautauqua features of the work. This year, for the first time, the Arches were erected and graduates of '89, as well as many former graduates of the C.L.S.C., passed through the Golden Gate.

The Normal department registered more students than any previous year. The Senior class was instructed by the Rev. C. M. Stuart; the Bible section, the Rev. H. G. Jackson; the Teachers' section, the Rev. H. W. Bolton. Graduating exercises of this department were held. Short speeches were made by representatives of each class; and prizes and diplomas presented.

At the Devotional Hour the Rev. W. H. Holmes gave a series of twelve carefully prepared Bible readings on the subject of the Redemption.

Among the speakers were Bishops Ninde and Fitz Gerald, Dr. J. P. D. John, J. M. Foster, the Rev. R. McIntyre, and G. W. Platt.

The new features of the year were schools in Photography and Microscopy. A special building was provided for their work, and it was filled to overflowing with enthusiastic students. The devotees of microscopy included many school teachers desirous to learn enough of it to use in their own work.

The Round Tables were inspiring. At some of the meetings the members gave their "experiences" in the form of written reports.

On Recognition Day services were held under the auspices of The Chautauqua Illinois Union. The address of the day was by Dr. H. G. Jackson. The Assembly graduated thirty-one persons, nineteen of whom were present. A Camp-Fire was held and speeches made by Dr. Patten, the Superintendent of the Assembly, and by others.

The work at Lake Bluff seems to be shaping in the direction of Summer Schools for teachers in the line of Science, Art, and Language.

Lakeside, Ohio. A large increase of attendance over previous years is reported from this session which was held from July 22 to August 4.

The usual work was done in the Boys and Girls' meetings, Normal classes, Primary Teachers' Conferences, under the direction of the Superintendent, the Rev. B. T. Vincent, aided by the Rev. H. M. Bacon, D. D., the Rev. C. W. Taneyhill, Mrs. B. T. Vincent, and others. Elocutionary instruction and kindergarten class work were added this year and were successful. Congresses were held in the interests of general church work and special Sunday-school advancement. The Sunday-schools, one under the superintendency of the Rev. W. F. McMillen, and the other under that of Mr. W. M. Day, were models of order and of instructive value.

The sermons by Bishop Vincent, the Rev. Drs. Buckley, McGaw, and Dowling were all able, and were listened to by great audiences.

The lecture course this year exceeded that of any previous year in brilliancy. Bishop Vincent, Joseph Cook, and Dr. Buckley were at their best in lectures and in answering the questions with which they were flooded. Other lecturers, such as Drs. Gunsaulus, Ladd, McGaw, Dowling, Grennell, Messrs. C. E. Stoakes, G. W. Edmundson, Leon H. Vincent, and Dr. L. B. Sperry gave able discourses on their respective themes.

The music was of an unusually fine character. Prof. B. M. Myers had charge, and with a most excellent band of wind and stringed instruments, able vocal soloists, among whom was Miss Genevra Johnson, of Chicago, and a well drilled choir, the best of work was done in this line.

The C. L. S. C. work greatly advanced. The presence of the Chancellor himself added great interest. He conducted Round Tables and Vesper Services. He delivered the oration on Recognition Day and presented the diplomas to the goodly number of the Class of '89 who were present. The procession was the largest in the history of Lakeside. The Arches were passed, the song and greetings followed; a vast audience filled the spacious Auditorium and thousands felt the uplifting influence of the Chancellor's able address. It is probable that a Hall will be built during the coming year as headquarters for the C. L. S. C. and Normal alumni; and enthusiasm for advancement in these and in all lines is great. These charming grounds with all their provision for the best recreative and culturing benefits are being more appreciated and crowded year after year, promising a brilliant and profitable future.

Long Beach, California. July 18 was observed as Recognition Day at Long Beach. The Rev. Dr. Hirst, President of the Pacific Coast C.L.S.C., the Rev. Dr. Sinex, of Monterey, the Rev. A. J. Marks, of Chicago, and Mrs. M. H. Field, Secretary of the Pacific Branch, addressed the graduating class. The floral decorations of the arches and platform were elaborate and beautiful.

At the Round Table held in the afternoon it was found that twelve circles were represented from California, three from Kansas, two from Michigan, Wisconsin, and Iowa, one from New York, Ohio, Pennsylvania, Massachusetts, and Oregon, twenty-six in all.

The committee of the circles of Southern California appointed to draw up resolutions regarding next year's Assembly, declared it their earnest wish that a yearly session be held at that place in co-operation with the officers of the C.L.S.C. of the Pacific Coast.

Mahtomedi, Minnesota. The Assembly this year was held from July 24 to August 6, and was divided into three parts: July 4 to 16 preliminary session with a Prohibition rally, July 4, with address by M.J. Fanning, a concert and elocutionary entertainment July 13, under the direction of Mrs. T. J. Preece; July 16 to 24, Bible School, under the auspices of the Y. M. C. A., with T. Gratton Guiness, of London, and others as instructors; July 24 to August 6 the Assembly, with the usual Normal, Primary Teachers, Physical Culture, Voice Culture, Elocution, Mental Training, and C. L. S. C. work, with lectures and concerts.

Dr. J. E. Gilbert and Miss Ida Anderson had charge of the Normal and Primary classes. Miss Esther Pugh, treasurer of the National W.C.T.U., directed the W.C.T.U. School of Methods. Prof. Schram conducted a Mental Training School. Mrs. T. J. Preece had classes in Voice Culture and Physical Training under the Delsarte system. Prof. Weston directed the Gymnasium and Swimming School. Mrs. C. H. Smith conducted a Jenness-Miller school.

The lecturers were Dr. Talmage, Peter F. Von Finkelstein, Prof. W. M. R. French, Prof. Freeman, Dr. L. G. Hay, the Hon. H. S. Fairchild, Prof. Hillman with the phonograph, and others. We also had Signor G. Vitale, the violinist, and the Mendelssohn Quartet, besides our local talent.

The C. L. S. C. interests were well taken care of, and at the close of the Assembly a movement for a Hall in the Grove was inaugurated with a subscription for nearly one-half the amount necessary to complete the building. The whole amount will be raised before January 1.

They made a little innovation in the manner of conducting the candidates through the Golden Gate on Recognition Day. They had four Arches with the Golden Gate in the last one. Through the first gate all Chautauquans passed; through the second only those of '89, '90, and '91; through the third only those of '89 and '90; and through the Golden Gate, of course, only '89's passed.

The C. L. S. C. interests are growing rapidly in Minnesota, and the Assembly management propose to push the work of circle formation this fall and winter.

Considering all the circumstances and the obstacles we have to contend with, we feel very much encouraged and are already planning for '90.

Warrensburg, Missouri. As the result of much energetic work the third session of the Missouri Assembly from July 17-27 was a great success. It reports that the state is awaking to the importance of the work done at this meeting.

Every morning four Normal classes were held. The Advanced Normal under the direction of Dr. Jesse B. Young; the

Bibical, Dr. Russell; the Young People's, Mrs. S. Knight; the Little Folks, Mrs. M.E. Steele. Fine work was done in these classes. A class chorus under the efficient direction of Dr. Herbert furnished excellent music. A series of lectures devoted to the study of English Literature was given to a large class, by Prof. J. W. Ellis, and was deservedly popular.

The following interesting lecturers were present: Dr. J. D. Hammon, the Hon. Will Cumback, Dr. Jesse Young, Dr. Willetts, Chas. W. Stevenson, the Rev. B. F. Boller. Dr. M. B. Chapman gave a number of interesting talks on missionary topics. A *Daily Assembly Herald* was published throughout the session and was found a great help in the work.

Round Tables were presided over by Dr. Russell, the Conductor of the Assembly, and things Chautauqua were discussed with much spirit. Dr. Russell, if possible, was more enthusiastic and earnest than ever before.

The Recognition Day services were led by Dr. Russell and the address given by Dr. Geo. P. Hays, on the subject "Sentiment in Education." Eight Missourians were given diplomas. A Camp-Fire closed the Assembly. Dr. Young was elected President of the Missouri Chautauqua Association. There are now two thousand Chautauquans in the state, and their organization is very efficient, and as a result circles are rapidly increasing.

Monona Lake, Wisconsin. The two weeks' session—July 23 to August 2—at the Monona Lake Assembly was characterized as most successful.

There were lectures from Dr. Raymond to the clergy; from Dr. Gladden on economic questions; popular lectures by Dr. Talmage, Dr. Gunsaulus, Joseph Cook, General Howard, Prof. De Motte, Frank Beard, and others. Dr. Palmer was the musical director. The Normal department was under the charge of Dr. J. A. Worden, and Mrs. Knox was at the head of the Primary Sunday-school work. Thus equipped, every division of the Assembly work was most ably and satisfactorily carried forward, and resulted in great good to all in attendance.

216

On Recognition Day the Class of '89, numbering fifty-one persons, passed between the open ranks of the undergraduate classes, through the Golden Gate and under the Arches, receiving the tributes of the flower misses. As the head of the Class of '89 came through the arches the choir sang "A Song of To-day." The class took seats in the temple and were formally recognized by Professor Shearer. Marching from the Rustic Temple to the Tabernacle, the graduating class took seats upon the platform with the officers and directors of the Assembly. The Rev. Joseph Cook, of Boston, delivered a thoughtful address, which was full of prophetic interpretations of the religious cause.

The prospects for the Class of '93 are reported as very good, and everything possible is to be done to increase the number of local circles in that region. The Hon. Elisha Coleman, of Fond du Lac, was chosen President of the State Association, and Miss Manning, of Oshkosh, Secretary.

Mountain Grove, Pennsylvania. August 7th, Recognition Day at Mountain Grove, was bright and cloudless, and Chautauquans were jubilant. At ten a.m. songs and responsive reading began the services. The Rev. B. B. Hamlin, D. D., of the Central Pennsylvania Conference was the speaker of the morning, his topic, "Learning to Read."

At one o'clock Chautauquans, preceded by flower girls, formed in a grand march, passing under the Arches according to rank, and filling the space assigned them in the audience. A quartet of vocal music followed the opening devotions, and the class poem was read by Prof. Will S. Monroe, a member of 1889. Rev. Dr. J. S. Judd, of Lewisburg, Pa., made the address to the class, and among other good things advised all to "learn *something* of *everything* and *everything* of *something.*"

He presented diplomas to twenty-four graduates who were recognized by loud applause and the Chautauqua salute. In the evening the first Camp-Fire was held and it was a brilliant success. Short services, followed by remarks from members, reports of committees, and spirited songs closed the first hour;

and then came the corn-roast, which delighted all. Several recruits for '93 were mustered in.

Mountain Lake Park, Maryland. The Chautauqua of the Alleghanies lies in that picturesque belt of mountain glades and atmospheric pleasures, three thousand feet above the sea, on the line of the Baltimore and Ohio Railroad between Baltimore and Wheeling. The great Park of nearly one thousand acres wooded by ancient white oaks is laid out in broad avenues, and studded everywhere with beautiful cottages. The water is abundant and delicious, the wild flowers bloom everywhere in nameless varieties, and the air is a positive and exhilarating tonic.

The session held from July 30 to August 12, was a success. The Normal work was maintained by the Revs. J. B. Van-Metre, George Elliot, and W. H. Leatherman. The Kindergarten, schools of Photography, Art, and Vocal Music were in the hands of eminent instructors.

Grand Army Day was graced with the presence of President Harrison.

Popular lectures were delivered by Drs. VanMetre, Scott F. Hershey, C. E. Bolton, Col. Alex. Campbell, and others.

Recognition Day was a prominent feature. The day itself was perfect. The C.L.S.C. Classes gathered under the big trees and had the march, under Marshal Armstrong. The Auditorium was handsomely decorated. The songs, responsive readings, and class poem, contributed to the occasion. The Rev. Mr. Elliot said words of recognition to the Class of '89 composed of ladies and gentlemen. The Rev. H. C. Pardoe delivered the graduating address on "The Trend of Anglo-Saxon Civilization during the present Century." The diplomas were presented, the Chautauqua salute given to the class, and blank applications for membership handed to each person in the audience. The day closed with a Camp-Fire, roasted corn, songs, etc.

The Round Table exercises during the Assembly were full of interest, and among other good things recommended the management to construct a real "Round Table" for 1890, and the organization of classes in botany and geology. President C. W. Baldwin is greatly encouraged at the outlook of the Assembly.

New England, Framingham, Mass. The tenth session of this Assembly was most prosperous. The program was brilliant, the classes well manned, and the C.L.S.C. largely represented. It was held from July 16-26.

One of the pleasantest days was that given to the children; exercises by Miss Lucy Wheelock's class took place in the Auditorium, followed by Dr. Dunning's lecture to children on "The New Pilgrim's Progress"; in the afternoon a children's meeting in charge of the W.C.T.U. was held; the evening concert was followed by a bonfire for the especial benefit of the little folks. Christian Endeavor and Framingham Normal Union Day had an appropriate program, with addresses by the Rev. F. E. Clark and the Rev. Dr. R. S. MacArthur. Gen. O.O. Howard and Gen. G. L. Swift were the orators of Grand Army Day. Musical Day closed the season, with a grand concert in the afternoon and another in the evening.

Four hundred thirty-one graduates marched to the Hall on Recognition Day where they were received by Principal Hurlbut. The commencement oration was then delivered by the Rev. Dr. Alexander McKenzie. Class reunions filled the remaining hours of the afternoon, and at six o'clock four hundred C.L.S.C. alumni sat down to a banquet in the Hall. Toasts and music added to the delights of the occasion. At a later hour a procession of ghostly beings took possession of the Auditorium and created much amusement until diplomas were awarded to them, when they disappeared as mysteriously as they came.

The Sunday-school Normal classes were instructed by Drs. Dunning and Hurlbut and the Rev. R. S. Holmes. Prof. Schauffler conducted the chorus drill. Meetings were held daily by the W.C.T.U. and a short address given at each one.

The list of popular lecturers was a long one, and included

Robert Nourse, Jahu DeWitt Miller, R. S. Holmes, and J. M. Buckley. The elocutionist George Riddle gave two very acceptable entertainments.

Ocean City, New Jersey. The Ocean City Chautauquans had a most delightful season together, from July 9-14. Every one present was interested and all were sorry when the end came.

Recognition Day will long be remembered as a most delightful occasion. Ten of the fourteen graduates were at the entrance to the Golden Gate under the arch of history. At the proper signal, the graduating class passed through the gate, and under the remaining arches of science, literature, and art. The last was adorned with the daisy, mingled with the evergreen. At the close of the Recognition Service, the C.L.S.C. march was conducted by the President. The Class of '89, followed by undergraduates and former graduates was the order. The Rev. C. B. Ogden, Class of '89, then read the class poem. The address was made before the graduates by the President, the Rev. J. S. Parker, and the C.L.S.C. diplomas were awarded by Mrs. L. H. Swain.

The Rev. C. B. Ogden represented in chalk the story of the Argonauts in their sail for the golden fleece. The subject was happily applied to the Class of '89, just graduating, who have attained the Golden Fleece of knowledge, the result of their four years' toil.

The following letter from Chancellor Vincent, written especially for the Ocean City Assembly, was read by the President:

"Denver and Rio Grande R.R., July 2, 1889.

Hearty greetings from the Wasatch Mountains on this glorious summer day to the members of the C.L.S.C. who gather for rest, rejoicing, and refreshing by the shores of the Atlantic!

"Amidst the glories of nature, as revealed by the side of the restless sea, or on the summits of the towering hills, we Chautauquans think of Him to whom we give all glory, and from whom we receive all grace, grace fuller and wider than the ocean, and loftier far than any mountains.

"To Him let us open our intellects that He may fill them with His wisdom, and our hearts that He may flood them with His love.

Yours in C.L.S.C. bonds,

John H. Vincent."

"The Lighting of the Camp-Fire," a special service prepared by the President, and followed by the usual Camp-Fire service, was made doubly attractive by the lighting of the fires by three young ladies, who gave appropriate selections.